# Spent

A Memoir by
**Antonia Crane**

A Barnacle Book 🐦 Rare Bird Books

THIS IS A GENUINE BARNACLE BOOK

A Barnacle Book | Rare Bird Books
453 South Spring Street, Suite 531
Los Angeles, CA 90013
abarnaclebook.com
rarebirdbooks.com

FIRST HARDCOVER EDITION

Portions of this book have been previously published in
*Black Clock, Diverse Voices Quarterly, Frequencies, Longreads,
The Moment: Six-Word Memoirs, The Rumpus, Rumpus Women,
Slake: Los Angeles, The Weeklings, The Whistling Fire,* and *Word Riot.*

Printed in Canada
Set in Goudy Old Style
Distributed in the U.S. by Publishers Group West

10 9 8 7 6 5 4 3 2 1

Publisher's Cataloging-in-Publication data

Crane, Antonia.
    Spent : a memoir / by Antonia Crane.
    p.cm.
    ISBN 978-1-940207-06-3

1. Crane, Antonia. 2. Stripteasers—United States—Biography. 3.
Mothers and daughters.   I. Title.

PN1949.S7 C73 2013
792.7/028/092 —dc23

*for Marilyn Rose DeWitt, my mother,*
*in honor of her strength and beauty*

*"Never underestimate the fury of a small town girl."*
—Romy Suskin

# Part 1

*"How sexy she is."*

# 1

*J*T WAS CHRISTMAS NIGHT, and Kara and I had a client at The Four Seasons in Beverly Hills— the type of place Britney Spears and Paris Hilton would smear foie gras on rice crackers and get shitfaced on Cristal, only they weren't there. We were. A mirrored elevator dumped us off on the fourth floor, where we were getting paid to meet a pale guy with silver hair and get him off. Kara knocked on the door after checking my teeth for lipstick stains. A tall man with bloodshot eyes ushered us into the suite. His skin hung on him like meat before it's tossed down the garbage disposal. "You're so amazing. Such beautiful souls," he said. "There's so much love. So much love," he said. He reached for us with forearms covered in red splotchy patches. *What's wrong with him? Eczema?* I thought, and noticed the fruit bowl piled high with figs and pears. I hadn't eaten. I hadn't even brushed my teeth. I spit out my sugar-free gum, ripped open a fig and bit into the goo.

I hugged him but it was an executive embrace. We barely touched. He said he was an attorney. *Like Dad*, I thought, wriggling out of the air hug to face him. He was a tower of white flesh, covered in tiny scabs. "We're your Christmas presents," I said.

Before Mom died, her tanned skin stretched away from her bones after all the chemo and radiation. Her strong solid arms shrunk. Her legs, shapely from years of horseback riding, withered away. I wanted to hug her, but it hurt her too much. She'd been in bed for weeks and winced when I reached for her. I could lie beside her, but only if I didn't move. She had a feeding tube in her stomach through a hole in her side. Around the hole were red sores and chafed skin. Sometimes the hole got infected. When that happened, we took trips to the hospital for intravenous antibiotics. The feeding tube was like an alien vacuum cleaner attachment: a thick rubber tube and a sac half-filled with thick, orange, liquid vitamin-syrup that flowed into her. When that sac was almost empty, it beeped like a garbage truck backing up. After the feeding tube, she never ate solids again.

When she was asleep her eyelashes fluttered. That's how I knew she was alive.

When her cancer returned after a brief remission, I started stripping again. I never thought I'd go back, but I always did. This was the fifth time. Girls I knew binged on cupcakes and cocaine when holes were punched through their hearts as the people they loved died; others went shopping. I walked into strip clubs, casinos, and hotels, and offered my body to strangers for money. Not my whole body, just certain parts. It was a relief to be touched by cash—just a few hundred bucks could soothe me. Maybe I'd make my rent. Maybe I'd get killed. What was important was the feel of it.

I was pushing forty and was short on my rent with no prospects. My friend Kara contacted me on Facebook after Pleasures, the strip club where I'd been working, shut down. I remembered her from a party in San Francisco, years ago. She carried a guitar around a room lit up by twinkling red pepper lights strung up the wall and over bookshelves.

As a sex worker, I'd met hundreds of women over the years, and although I don't remember their names, I remember certain songs they always danced to and the smell of cheap peach lotion on their skin. I remember drops of sweat on their spine as they stepped offstage and the way they hastily tied the bow on a pink lacy bra they had worn to death. I remember the way their ribcage moved as they gyrated on laps, a mole on her chin, freckles on her thighs. At that party, I remembered Kara's vacant blue eyes and her soft voice answering "yeah" to any question I asked. I didn't know if she was a sex worker back then, but her roommate was. Kara smoked nervously and had a chip on her right tooth, but grinned wide anyway. So when I met her at her loft downtown, she chain smoked while I stared at the chip on her right tooth and wondered why she wanted to help me. Her proud smile reminded me of Mom. I talked about my money worries.

"I can help you," she said. She suggested we put up an add on an escort site for massage. "I'm no massage therapist," I said. She promised to show me the happy ending ropes. I figured no matter how much porn guys consumed, touch was something computer screens hadn't yet replaced. So, we took cheesy pictures on her phone and uploaded them onto the site.

She texted her regular client Dennis and set up a meeting. He was first in a long line of clients in my hand job life with Kara—our shoulders touched in elevators after she chucked her cigarette into the grass. I smelled smoke on her fingers and chewed my gum fast in tense moments while walking through empty lobbies and hallways looking at numbers, counting in whispers.

My own body went through the motions of sex work while my mom's body shriveled from bile duct cancer.

In those feeding tube days, I dreamed of Mom's voice on the answering machine, saying, "Would you just look at this spaghetti squash? Big as pumpkins and so early!" She spoke until my answering machine cut her off and I jerked awake.

In the beige penthouse suite, I got undressed except for my shoes, bra, and fishnets. Kara liked to be naked. Dennis wrapped his long scaly arms around us. "Such sweet energy," he said. Grisly black hair covered his chest and sprouted from his ears. We walked over to the California King mattress where he lay on his back, a beached whale in soft sand with his belly up. The white sheets were expensive. "Are you married?" Kara asked. She had her methods with married men. She wanted to teach them to bring their wives to a massive orgasm. It was stuff she learned in a sex cult in Northern California. She crammed a rose quartz crystal in his left palm.

"She passed away two years ago," he said. He didn't look sad. He closed his eyes, and the soft pillow caved with weight-memory foam. "You're sooo amazing," he said. His voiced reminded me of soft crying. I wondered if he missed his wife. I felt sorry for him and had an impulse to kiss his neck, scales or no scales.

"Do you mind if I dim these lights?" I asked. I was a stripper first and foremost, so I made a big production out of taking off my clothes. The lighting had to be right. I unfastened my bra, twirled it, and tossed it onto the floor; then I joined Kara, who was on top of him already, with her legs straddling him. I sat behind her.

"You're wearing too many clothes," she said to me while facing him. Her palms were flat on his chest as she smeared him with coconut oil. That's when I saw his feet. His big toes were rotting off at the tips, the skin like chewed jerky. His arches were flat as skis and the rotten skin spread to his calves. Red bruises traveled up his legs. He had scabs the size of fat ticks on both of his ankles. *Jesus*, I thought. *Leprosy*.

Kara kept the fantasy going. She talked dirty. "I feel like you're inside me," she said. Her hands were behind her back now, pointing to his junk. This was her signal for me to look at him more closely, which I did. "What's your fantasy?" she asked him. I scooped my hand into the plastic tub of coconut oil and rubbed the grease into the deep wet creases of his stretch-marked, blubbery thighs. I moved my face to his crotch to get the skinny on his condition.

"I'm a kid in art class and my teacher calls me into her office," he said. "She tells me to take my clothes off. She photographs me. Then she demands I play with myself but I hear girls giggling." Kara giggled. I moved down to massage his calves, careful to avoid open sores and flaking skin. I saw that his cock had tiny red pustules on it. My slimy hand held it in a firm grip. "Will you suck it?" He asked with his eyes still closed, mouth open, still as death.

"You have some red spots and it looks like...well, genital warts," I said.

"The doctor says it's just age. Promise," he said.

"And, I have a blood disease."

*He thinks we're stupid whores*, I think, no longer feeling much sympathy for him: Blood Cancer, Gangrene, Diabetes, HIV. For the clients, it's never just about the boner. They want to tell their secrets to a naked girl who isn't invested in them. Secrets like a preference to be paddled or wanting to be told "Don't move" while a thermometer slides into their asshole. Secrets like popping Vicodin when bosses and wives think they're clean and sober, or being unhappily married and unable to leave because of guilt and children. I hold their secrets while they hold me and call me Tess, Candace, Chelsea, or Nicole. Anonymity is part of the allure for both of us. While our skins slide together, they want to feel desired, they want to get off, and, an hour later, they want me to leave with their money and secrets tucked in my purse.

With the money I imagined buying golf balls for my dad and a Target gift card for my brother, but I knew this money would go towards rent. "A promise isn't enough," Kara said, forehead to forehead with Dennis. She had a way of saying hard things so they landed like soft bunnies. Out of my mouth the same words would castrate a man.

"Do you have a condom?" he asked, stroking his cock. Only twenty minutes had passed, but it felt like hours. I massaged his balls, and my armpits began to sweat.

"No." Kara stared at his closed eyes. She was into energy work and the shaman thing. She said I worked too hard and I don't think she was wrong but it was a service job to me. He opened his eyes, ending his trance. "There's more in it for both of you," he said.

"Double." Kara gave me a nod. I sprung up and leapt to the bathroom, where there were billion thread count towels and downy robes hanging from the door, petite glass bottles of Evian, and guest soaps worth more than my car.

I wiped my gooey hands on a monogrammed towel then took two types of condoms, one with lube and one without. The best one would be without, because it wouldn't slip or slide off. *Four hundred bucks*, I thought. *Almost half my rent.* I unwrapped it slowly and slid it onto our man. I looked into Kara's blank blue eyes and our tongues met in circles around the latex condom. I tasted the sour plastic of new tires, party balloons, and hospital gloves and wondered if his wife died of the same blood disease that he had, and if they had ever spent Christmas in this hotel.

# 2

ROWING UP, I LIKED dirt. My backyard was a wet and mossy redwood forest. In the summer, the fog hung like strips of cotton on the branches. When the sun melted the mist, the fog dripped from the tips. Heading North on the 101 towards Arcata or South towards Fortuna were thick layers of sequoias— shades of dark green giants swaying above brown-red trunks as far as one could see. The shadows they cast brought a quick and quiet night. There's no silence like Humboldt.

The grassy hill where I played was green and lush. Like a lot of kids, I spent hours constructing forts out of old redwoods. I'd find a stump and use branches to form a shelter from which I watched the banana slugs leave slimy trails below. I would pick huckleberries and blackberries and dig into the soil to snatch slim carrots from the garden. I threw stones in the pond. At nine, I pretended I was an Indian princess hiding from cowboys. I didn't want to hide too well because I wanted them to find me, put me on their horses, and ride away with me. Horsetails lined a creek that glistened with silver rocks. Rays of sun reached through the branches, but the trees cooled the creek's bright glow, turning it orange and gentle and still.

Out front, I ran up the ivy-coated hill to a spongy moss-covered stump and pulled myself up. My pretend cowboys never showed up, so I roller skated down the hill in front of my house pretending to be Olivia Newton-John in *Grease*, after she got slutty. I'd roll too fast until I was scared of crashing, then collapse into spit-covered ivy. Soaked, I'd run into the forest and climb over the broken redwood fence and into another yard where I was chased by the neighbor's mean goat, but it never stopped me from stealing their boat and paddling in their pond or from taking a ride on their rope swing. I played alone, and the trees stayed still and watched.

I was surrounded by shadows, bark, and moss. The Pacific Ocean was violent and windy. In high school, on rare sunny days, I'd cut class and drive to Samoa Beach to sit on cold sand. Almost no one went near the ocean without a wetsuit—if I so much as stuck a toe in the water, I squealed. Seagulls flew overhead and pelicans built huge nests on top of electrical posts. The crab boats were docked. Samoa Beach smelled like dead fish and bird shit and home.

The summer Mom died, I got pulled over by a cop for flipping an illegal U-turn to park at the beach and stare out at the ocean. While he spoke to me, I watched waves crash. I wished I could ignore him, but instead I fished my papers out from the glove box.

"You just crossed a double yellow," the cop said.

"My mom is dying three houses down. I'm from here." I pointed in the direction of her house. But now I can't remember if that happened right before or right after she died, because that's what death does to memory. Before and after was one day. She was carried off in a big van without her pink and green striped socks because I took those. Wind whipped my face.

The cop didn't write me a ticket.

"Get your head together," he said.

When he was gone, I walked down to the water, sat on a wet log, and stared at the tide. I wanted to be somewhere else that day—somewhere with my mom, laughing while spreading chocolate frosting on a sheet cake for one of her women's organization meetings. The ocean tide ripped moss and branches with a fast, cold thrust; it pounded as she drifted away. I wanted to sit with her in the sunshine, both of us reading books and munching on her M&M's. I wanted her to be home when I returned with the truck.

On the wet log, in front of icy waves, I remembered things I was told: I was born on the darkest night in November with no moon. Mom wanted a girl so bad she was sure I'd be a boy. She only had boys' names in mind: Anthony. Joel.

She was flummoxed when I was a girl. The name she gave me came from one of those seventies name books. Most of the names in our family lacked spice—Susan and Jen and Steve, with sounds that hung around the front teeth and barely troubled the tongue at all. But Mom wanted something that could be shortened, something with more syllables. So she picked Antonia, which means priceless treasure. Aunt Lou was appalled that my mother had chosen an Italian name. In pictures taken that day, Aunt Lou frowned like a troll, but Mom's toothpaste-commercial smile canceled all that out.

ONE WEEK BEFORE MOM died, she had said, "Come look at photo albums with me. I'm the only one who knows who these people are." We never got the chance, and I took the albums with me back to Los Angeles. She'd been right. Who were these hillbillies? The people between the sticky film pages were a gristly clan of Irish, French, and Algonquin country bumpkins with big hands and dirty feet. They carved smiley faces into their blackberry pies, collected coins, dug ditches, and kept bees.

I would never know who any of these people were. But there I was in a faded Polaroid, puckered, pink, and ugly—wrapped in a fuzzy blue blanket, not a boy.

# 3

ON THE DAY HE left, Dad said, "You'll always be my little girl," and I followed him onto the porch, watching. I was ten. I tasted rot on my tongue as he walked to his car and drove away. My mouth was dry from hanging open, and I couldn't cry. I stood frozen on the porch facing the empty driveway for a long time while Mom wailed beside me.

She was standing at the front door of our house one minute, sturdy and tough, then collapsed at the knees like a flimsy doll as he drove away. Alan picked her up, carried her into the living room, and set her down on the fuzzy brown couch. She sat there wailing "Nooo..." and stayed like that for hours, getting skinnier every second. Drool spilled out of her mouth and soaked the couch.

Dad took up residence in a fleabag hotel on Broadway for a while, before moving in with a curvy redhead. Then he bought a cabin a half hour away, in a town that had one church, one gas station, and one grocery store. It was decided I'd stay with Mom, and my brother would move in with him. When I visited on weekends, I swept the country store with a big wood broom in exchange for all the Twix bars and Reese's Peanut Butter Cups I wanted. This was three years before I learned how to throw it all up from the girls in Jazzercize class.

Alan was my football-playing, pot-smoking big brother, and I missed him. He was girl crazy and constantly played air guitar to Mr. Bungle, Slayer, and Iron Maiden. He knew all the words and stomped around the house singing them loudly. I looked up to him even though he was always in trouble for selling pot and stealing Dad's car. He took pills and grew pot in his closet. I didn't even know exactly what that meant, only that it was a delicious secret from Mom and Dad. After the divorce, Dad bought him a sparkling brown truck, and he wasn't around much after that.

My dad had left us right after his law office got robbed. "He rigged it to steal your inheritance," Mom said. "Your father said he had a feeling something was wrong at the office, but your father wouldn't know a feeling if it bit him in the face."

I'll never know the truth, but I know what I saw—Mom turned to jelly.

IT TOOK A WHILE for Mom to get used to her new life. After months of denial, she grew comfortable with being angry, then, finally, sad. She drank more, which didn't help, started smoking More menthols, and threw herself at her work and her women's organizations. She yelled at me when I didn't pay attention to her and sometimes dragged me to her meetings or on dates where I would be bored stiff. I'd sit and listen to the radio and memorize all the songs that played on Humboldt's one rock station.

The changes seemed to affect Dad less. He seemed upbeat, even happy. I wasn't sure I recognized him. He stopped smoking. He looked younger and more tan. Once, he picked me up to go see Alan play football in a town about an hour north of Humboldt. The redwoods swayed as we zipped along in Dad's post-divorce blue and silver 280-ZX. He explained that I was going to be introduced to Jill, the new woman he was dating. On the side of the road, a redwood cracked and fell as we approached it.

I screamed. He sped up over eighty, and we raced below it, barely missing it.

The giant tree collapsed onto the freeway, blocking the van behind us; its branches like wild fingers. My dad, the hero race car driver still wearing his suit and tie from a day in court.

"I'm the best damn driver you've ever seen," he said, then rolled down the window. "Hurricane winds, my ass." When we reached Crescent City, a tiny suburban town on the northernmost tip of California, it was pitch black because the electricity was out. Windows were cracked in the Denny's as we drove by. Pieces from roofs were blowing along on the sidewalk. More redwoods swayed in the wind and landed on rooftops. We arrived in front of a small blue house in the ravaged town. When the front door opened, a thin, pretty woman with soft brown eyes greeted us in a very high-pitched voice which could barely be heard with the crashing chimes outside. She looked like a fragile bird in the raging storm, and her three-year-old daughter held her hand in the dark. Alan's football game was canceled, and he went home with the rest of his team on the bus, so it was just my dad's pretty new girls and me.

One restaurant was open. Dad, Jill, her four-year old daughter, and I sat in a booth, and I worried about the windows exploding from the pressure outside. I squeezed in next to him and shook. "Dad, did you rob your own office?" I asked.

Wind whipped through the restaurant and whistled. Jill's eyes avoided mine while she sat up straight and cleared her throat. "What did you just ask me?" Dad asked. My insides felt stuck together with gum while his new girlfriend and her baby voice slowly peeled us apart for good.

# 4

*I* MUST HAVE BEEN ABOUT ten when my mom called me sexy because I was in uniform. My navy blue pants were so tight I couldn't bend over without sucking in my breath. My shirt was white and stiff with a floppy eyelet collar and plastic white buttons. I didn't need a training bra yet. Under my shirt was a soft white tank top with dark blue roses on it. My mom grabbed my waist with her hands and squeezed tight and stretched her fingers around until her thumbs and middle fingers met. I figured she was playing the baby fat game where she pinched my sides and cackled like a scarlet macaw. "God! You're so sexy," she said. I was embarrassed but not sure why. "Look!" she called out to my big brother. "How sexy she is."

"Mom, don't," I said. Alan sprinted downstairs with his Walkman on.

Whatever sexy was, it must have been the worst thing in the world, like being boiled alive with my nerves still intact, or the best thing ever, like winning a game of kick-the-can. I wanted to swat her hands away so I could breathe, but I held my breath so I could glow in her grasp. She saw me as sexy, and that meant I existed. It meant I existed even after Dad left. It meant I could breathe again.

"Alan said I'm fat," I said, wriggling away from her.

"You're not fat, honey, you're chunky. It's sexy." I didn't want to be chunky. I wanted to look like Christie Brinkley, have a twenty-five inch waist, and marry David Bowie. I was haunted by fat, always pinching the blubber on my hips. I hated mirrors. I compared my thighs to the skinny girls in Jazzercise whose bodies were sharp points of perfection. I was tall with oddly long, flat feet. I was the opposite of them: loud and thick and wore all blue instead of pink. With my dad's muscular thighs, I was too fat for ballet. I willed myself to be skinny, but the only diet I saw work was divorce. After Mom's friends got divorced, they got thin. I didn't want to wait that long.

I BEGGED MY MOM to let me watch *Family*, a show about a troubled teenager, which came on at 10:00 P.M., past bedtime. I hadn't noticed it happening, what with the divorce and the new circumstances, but Kristy McNichol was my idol, and I'd become obsessed with her. Kristy played the teenage star, and I loved her feathered hair and the chocolate chip mole on her lip. And I increasingly loved her tight bell-bottomed jeans and the blue satin jacket that unzipped to show a tight baseball T-shirt. Kristy played Buddy, a tomboy whose legs dangled from the swing set on the front lawn; a lip glossed, tough girl with mental problems and a gap in her teeth. I thought about her in *Little Darlings* when I masturbated on my pillow. I read rumors in the tabloids that she was a bipolar lesbian, and it took a couple of consultations with a dictionary to figure out what that meant. This made her seem hotter to me. She was the most beautiful woman on earth and had the best body on television, hands down. It didn't occur to me to question my own sexuality; what I felt for Kristy felt right, and it didn't interfere with my interest in boys. It wasn't in the least confusing. I preferred being with my girlfriends. I took baths with them in Mom's Avon scented bubble bath and slept in their beds with them, praised their soft skin, played with their hair, and borrowed their clothes. I didn't think about the term "bisexual" or apply it to myself—at least not yet. Sexuality felt like a space I stepped into and out of like a mud puddle. I wanted to be chased by boys in the worst way and my body ached when they ignored me. But when they chased me I got scared and quiet, my face flushed, and my body heated up. I wanted to be chased by boys, but I wanted to kiss girls. I admired their strength and soft pillow-like beauty. I wanted to keep their secrets and sleep next to them. I glided between sexes and needed them both. I didn't hate one and run to the other in refuge. I loved both and rejected both—two forces tugged inside me, and I didn't yet know enough to be ashamed.

IT WAS DURING A commercial break of *Family* that I first stuck my finger down my throat. I'd read about bulimia in *Seventeen*. Bulimia was the ticket to losing weight, at least according to the girls in Jazzercize class. My blonde, small-boned Mormon cheerleader friends did it, and their moms all looked like Loni Anderson on WKRP in Cincinnati. I polished off a gallon of Rocky Road ice cream and worked my way through a bag of Zingers then I ran bathwater extra loud and puked until my knuckles had red cuts and blisters from my teeth. Loni Anderson's wide bleached smile mocked me from the television after I washed the slime from my mouth. I thought about kissing Kristy. I wondered if she was born with a perfect body or if she too stuck her finger down her throat five times a day.

I liked having a secret, even then. It's something that hasn't changed. Other peoples', as well as my own. One effective way to keep my secrets was to tell on other girls. I called Janine Elm's parents and told them she was bulimic because it took the focus off of me. "You did the right thing, honey. She could die," Mom said, and made me a roast beef sandwich, which I later threw up.

Kristy McNichol was sexy, but Madonna was the sexiest, prancing around in fishnets with messy, blonde hair and eyeliner. I wanted her to guide me, so I memorized all of her songs.

By fourteen, my boyfriend was a varsity football player who looked exactly like Sylvester Stallone and I was a cheerleader with pizza-puke breath. I was a couple years younger than Jeff and was desperately in love with him. I even made a heart-shaped wooden sign that said so and screwed it to a telephone pole near his house on Valentine's Day. He broke up with me shortly after. I barfed my way through high school, chasing an impossible standard of beauty. I embraced and fought the cravings inside my body—stuffing it down, then throwing it up.

Both men and boys began paying attention to me, and I began to pay attention to what worked, to what kept them interested. I became an outrageous flirt, destined for laps across America. I was an inevitable stripper—barfing, teasing, aching to be seen.

# 5

WHILE I BINGED AND purged, Mom stopped eating and joined a volleyball team. She'd become skinny like a model. I could tell by the way she smiled at herself in the full-length mirror and swerved when she walked that she liked her legs. Her brown polyester skirt floated inches above her knees. According to her, everyone said she had terrific legs, and it was true. She never worked out at a gym or walked farther than down the driveway to the car and from the car to her office, so when she joined a volleyball team I was surprised. I'd never seen her wear white socks, just Hanes control top pantyhose that made her shapely legs shimmer and glide.

The volleyball team was where she met Chris, a hunky postman she hastily moved into our house after they had been dating for a few months. He had a Tom Selleck moustache and wore little, blue terrycloth shorts. He spent a lot of time in the garage building stuff: bookshelves, cabinets, and canoes. He woke up at 5:00 A.M. to deliver mail then came home and napped from about 3:00 P.M. until 5:00 P.M.

You didn't want to wake him up.

In our house, there was a bar downstairs with stools where Mom and Chris gulped yellow booze with three ice cubes from rocks glasses. Mom liked to swish hers around in a circle, making the cubes clack against her glass.

The sound reminded me of galloping horses. Mom loved to tell stories about being a little girl when she got drunk. "My brother got everything," she growled. "He could go out and do whatever he wanted. I had to get perfect grades and do all the housework. Do his homework. The happiest day of my life was going to ride Kathy's horse. I wanted to stay there and brush the horse and ride her horse, Bo, forever. I didn't care when he kicked my teeth out. I wanted a horse more than anything in the world." I wanted to give her a horse—anything she wanted. I hoped Chris would.

THE FIRST NIGHT IT happened, I closed my eyes in bed and listened to them argue. Mom's bedroom was directly above mine. I heard a loud thud. I recognized the sound of her body being slammed against the bedroom door. Mom kept whimpering, "Please stop." His feet stomped across the ceiling like a monster. I expected to hear a laugh track, but there was only yelling. He threw things that hit the walls. I imagined the lamp and the alarm clock splitting into shards.

Outside, the wind blew the redwoods hard. Branches creaked and snapped. The sound was like limbs breaking. I liked the outside sounds better than the inside ones. I opened my window and inhaled damp forest air. I thought about crawling out the window and grabbing the tire swing and slowly lowering myself down like Wonder Woman.

I heard feet running: heavy long strides above me like Sasquatch.

"If I can't sleep, no one's sleeping!" Chris turned on all of the lights and televisions in the house full blast. The stereo blared Kenny Rogers' "The Gambler." I knew all the words because my mom played that album nonstop in her green Volvo while she smoked her menthols. We would sing along loudly to "She Believes In Me." My eyes were open and I mouthed the words, but I held my breath and didn't stir. If I was very still, I figured they would stop.

Mom appeared in the doorway and sat on my bed. I'm not sure why. She had a cut on her lip that was bleeding through the Kleenex. I worried about her pretty smile. "I love you," she said from beneath the tissue and pet my leg. She was drunk.

In a few minutes, she left, then the lights, televisions, and stereo were shut off, and it was quiet apart from the wind. I was wide awake, so I turned on my black and white television and watched the most beautiful woman

I've ever seen in an elaborate white wedding dress walk in front of thousands of fancy guests. She stood close to a man with a big nose. He wore a stiff military jacket and had delicate hands. The woman was slim with soft blonde, feathered hair. The train on her dress was at least twenty-five feet long. I watched them say vows and kiss with formal elegance. The woman had golden skin. Her expression was gentle and prim. I wanted to look exactly like her. I studied her hair. I had no idea who they were, but the news announcers told me they were Lady Diana and Prince Charles.

The mornings after Mom and Chris fought, I watched her dab beige Avon makeup on her bruised eyes and smear frosted pink lipstick on her swollen lips before she went to work as a legal secretary. I followed her around and spelled words out loud for my spelling test as she admired herself in the mirror and sprayed Charlie perfume on her delicate neck. "Res-tau-rant." She reached for a string of beads the color of dried blood and put them around her neck. She took them off and chose a string of rose quartz, lavender, pink, and white orbs instead. "R-E-S-T-R-A-N-T."

"Wrong." She dug around for her matching lavender quartz earrings. "R-E-S-T-A-R-N-T." *She'll yell if I screw up again.* "Three syllables. You're missing a syllable. Pay attention."

All of her suits were color coordinated. She used to match her taupe vests with blouses that she would tuck into her nylons. Her suits were polyester because, she said, "They don't need ironing." She was a joiner of women's groups, an attender of luncheons, and president of AAUW (American Association of University Women). She was a member of DAR (Daughters of the American Revolution). She was treasurer of her class, and she drank with sorority sisters. She never missed a day of work. She cooked and cleaned. She was stern, capable and delicate, like Lady Di, I think. Her boyfriend beat her, and she loved him. I loved him, too. He paid attention to me and liked the same music that I liked. We sang along with the radio in the car. His raspy, deep, voice in harmony with mine as we drove. "He's the love of my life," Mom used to say.

The night Mom's yelling became screaming I called the cops from my yellow phone, then climbed out of the window and walked up the cement stairs alongside the house. I watched Mom convince the cops dressed in a women's organization voice and matching blouse. "Everything is fine," she said. The cops talked softly and wrote things down on small pads of paper, then they left and it was just me in the moonlight, spying on her from the side of the house. I felt guilty. Mom went inside again, but I walked down the hill and through my neighbor's garage into my best friend, Kate's, house. Kate's mom, Rose, was a second mom to me. Rose was standing in the dark kitchen drinking a glass of wine. When I told her about the yelling, she said, "It's just water off a duck's back."

I didn't believe her. I figured she just wanted me to go away. It was a school night. I went outside and walked the streets of my small town in the moonlight, then snuck back into my window at sunrise like nothing happened.

# 6

*I* LOST MY VIRGINITY DURING a blackout, in a summer cabin near the Eel River.

By fourteen, I'd found alcohol. I never liked the taste; I just drank to get gone. Usually, the way it happened was a friend had a party, and we all showed up and guzzled their parents' stash. I drank until the burn melted my throat and I fell down. Those summers were foggy and cold, but it got warmer an hour South of Eureka in Garberville, the notorious pot mecca.

Kate's family had a summer cabin in the hills of Garberville. The first time I went I must have been about seven years old. I got sick from Kate's Mom's white spaghetti, but I think I was just homesick and scared. It was my first sleepover out of town and I missed Mom.

Kate had a big family with two older sisters who were Gods to me. They listened to Top 40 music, had boyfriends, knew how to bake cookies from scratch, and curled their hair like the girls in *Seventeen* magazine. They baby-oiled their tanned curves, wore pink and turquoise string bikinis, and bought expensive sunglasses from a department store in Santa Rosa with their babysitting money. They did ballet. I wanted Kate's family: her sisters and her mom who stayed home and cooked. My mom preferred men and things that were dangerous for her, like runaway horses, menthols, and raging men. Never mind the things that were quiet and safe. I was born with her same cravings and tendencies. When I put myself at risk, I felt closer to her, daring her to keep me safe. I did this knowing she wanted to more than anything, but she didn't know how.

AFTER I ADOPTED MYSELF into Kate's family, I got invited to Redway instead of going to the poor camp. Redway looked a lot like a campground and had rope swings that hung from redwoods. There was a dirt trail with wobbly wooden steps leading to the Eel River. In the car with Kate and her sisters, we sang commercial jingles like, "Don't give me that so-so soda, the same old Coca-Cola, I wanna rock and roll-a." We'd go back and forth like that, first Shasta then Tab, "For beautiful people."

To become a beautiful person, I barfed two or three times per day. I had red sores on the knuckles of my right hand from rubbing against my teeth. They're now little white scar-slivers where I picked the scabs and didn't let them heal. No matter how much I barfed, no matter how much Jazzercise I did, I was never going to be skinny, but it wasn't only about the weight. Bulimia was about control, which I was always on the brink of losing.

I barfed up every meal and guzzled hard alcohol with Diet Sprite. Alcohol was easy enough to find— the fully-stocked bar downstairs in my house, where neighborhood drunks hung out and played liar's dice with me, and sometimes Alan, when he was avoiding Dad and his new family. Mom and Chris kept the whiskey flowing, so I poured the gin or rum into a glass and added water to the bottle to fill the gap I left. They'd never notice the difference. I drank alone in the dark, keeping both barfing and booze secret.

At Kate's cabin, I was nervous to barf because I was worried she'd hear me and get upset or send me home. It was close quarters, so I snuck into the bathroom when it was empty and the rest of Kate's family was at the river, worried they would hear me retch. It was close quarters and I had little privacy, while at home I was left alone and there were several bathrooms where I could hide, run water, and puke my heart out. No one was ever around.

With television as my very best friend, I knew every commercial by heart. I was delighted to chew Freshen-Up gum that exploded in my mouth and knew every word to every Blondie and Prince song. Singing was like praying. With music as my mouthpiece, Madonna and Prince expressed my emotions for me. I was spawned by MTV, absolutely brainwashed by Madonna's sloppy bawdiness and Catholic pageantry. I studied her songs, gyrated to

"Burning Up For Your Love," and stole gobs of plastic bracelets from Woolworth's that covered my forearms. I sported black lace fingerless gloves to hide the scars. I was determined to have sex, but I'd only kissed boys. Girls were easier to get close to, and although I thought about it, I didn't kiss them until later on. Since my mom wouldn't allow me to date until I was sixteen, I developed a knack for lying and sneaking.

By the time I was fourteen, I was already enjoying attention from boys, but I had no idea what to do about it. Kate and I went to private Catholic school together for the first seven years, until we decided that wearing uniforms sucked. Public schools had boys and fashion, punk kids and no mandatory mass. Our parents eventually caved to our pleas. In public school, the boys I flirted with pinched my butt and gave me mean looks. They nudged me, kissed me, then ran away.

Rudy Geraldi was an olive skinned dreamboat who made all us laugh. I had a terrible crush on him. He was tall and mature, seventeen years old with even teeth. Us girls—Kate, Sandy, Jolie, and I—planned a sleepover at Rudy's place while his family was away. We drank his parents' vodka and played music and danced around with our elbows out and our knees weak in the summer heat. I got shitfaced with Kate, and we got loud and ridiculous. I was a stupid, reckless drunk, singing my commercial jingles and dancing around, hating my body, but I barely remember this. I do remember the beds outside where we slept. They were old iron frames with striped mattresses that smelled like bug spray and suntan lotion. I wore turquoise and purple plaid preppy shorts and a sky blue Izod shirt. "Is this okay?" He asked. Tongues, lips, no bra. Shorts sliding down past my knees. The sky shimmered with blurry lights, like water with eyes. "You must be my Lucky Star," I said, moving my arms up in a sloppy cheerleader move.

"Are you sure?" Rudy asked. I remember the question but not the answer. Prince's "Little Red Corvette" played over and over, someone had put it on repeat and then passed out. His hair was fine and silky. I shrunk when he was on top of me, finally the thin girl I wanted to be—under a big black sky that was asking, "Are you sure?"

My tongue must have tasted rotten with vodka and my teeth rancid from puke. If there was pain, it was an echo of a Shasta soda pop commercial, a crinkle of tin. "I want a thrill, I want a wow, I want that taste I want it now." The music faded and the stars blurred. I remember the musty smell of damp Redwoods and little else. When I woke up, my head pounded. There was a bump the size of a walnut on the back of my head where I must have hit it against the headboard. I looked down. There was blood dripping down my legs, running down my thighs. Rudy was asleep next to me with his back to me. The mattress springs dug into my back. I found my crumpled T-shirt and pulled it over my naked body and went to find Kate and Sandy.

"What happened?" Sandy asked, seeing the blood.

"I think we did it," I said. "Please don't tell Kate." I was embarrassed, ashamed, and scared. I held my sore head in my hand. I found my plaid shorts under the bed. They were also bloody. I went inside the bathroom and watched my highlighted hair fall into the toilet water as I puked. I thought about Tab Cola, with just one calorie for beautiful people—like me. I felt light headed and held the toiled bowl sides to keep from falling. My head ached. I was losing weight. I rinsed my baggy, wrinkled, damp shorts in the sink. I could throw up, but I could never take it back. I reached for the pink can of Tab, swallowed it, and made Rudy my boyfriend until he wasn't.

# Part 2

*"Killing me."*

# 7

*I* MET THE ORCHID BREEDER at the coffee shop in Old Town, Eureka, which was packed with hippies and artists. I'd gotten out, away from my mom and stepdad and dad and was living on my own by seventeen. Being a barista was one of my many shit jobs, which led to another shit job: artist's model. Some of my customers hired me to pose nude for them—for an untaxed hourly wage—in studios and warehouses nearby where they painted or sketched. I stood or sat naked, and they collected money in a basket like church and gave it to me afterwards.

A squat man with a posture like he'd just had a prostate exam asked me for a small coffee. "You're fetching," he said. His shiny black hair hung in his bulging eyes. He brushed it away.

"Thanks." I handed him a white mug of burnt coffee. He gave me his business card, which read: Orchid Breeder. Painter.

"You should sit for me," he said.

I shoved the card in my sock. The café was packed, with a line out the door. Two craggy men in plaid flannel shirts played chess and camped out. Shop owners left with their trays of lattes and muffins and four local punks occupied their usual table.

"Will you turn the music up?" the one with spiky purple hair asked.

I walked in the back and turned up David Byrne's "The Catherine Wheel" and emptied the tip jar in my apron pocket. I had to pee.

I poured coffee grounds in the trash, wiped counters, and cut up blackcurrant scone samples. I popped one in my mouth. I needed to scratch together enough cash to get out of this cow town. I was feeling cramped and lonely. Maybe I needed to go to San Francisco where I could do what I want without being watched like a hawk by people who knew me my entire life. Ten bucks a day in coffee tips wasn't cutting it. I called the orchid breeder's number.

"Can you model for me tomorrow for a few hours?"

"How much?" I asked.

"Fifteen an hour," he said.

I met him in a dusty attic loft in Old Town, with creaky redwood beams and orange light spilling through the windows. I was about twenty. The orchid breeder was thirty-six with a fixed, tense expression and frog-like eyes that never blinked. He smoked cigars and painted on a canvas with a couple of skinny branches that he dipped in muddy red paint.

"Have you ever done acid?"

"Nope."

"How is that possible? A fetching girl like you?" He opened and shut the freezer and handed me a tiny, white piece of paper, which dissolved on my tongue. We spent the next several hours touching and kissing. I got lost standing up. Time became syrup I couldn't move through. My gut was empty. I loved every last minute of it.

That was how the affair started. Not with mutual attraction or interests—the married man had the yummy drugs; he had the drug that made everything perfect, not just acid. He bought perfect powdered speed by the quarter baggy and fed it to me off his red kitchen counter; it made my soul swim. Crank was the answer to a question I didn't know I had. It made me frantic and thin and euphoric. I snorted a line and soared skinless and weightless and looked down in a jagged disconnect. Did I mention speed made me skinny? Perfect.

The orchid breeder was married to a woman named Kayla. What I knew about Kayla was that she was delicate, pretty, and blonde. And that she had been raped. I didn't know what it meant to leave a wife, especially one who had been raped, but I'm sure Kayla still has a doll in my likeness with pins stuck through its eyes.

One afternoon, the orchid breeder called. He was puffing on a cigar and asked, "Do you want to come to San Francisco?" Of course I did. This hick town was tightening around my neck. The alcohol and bars and acid trips were making me late for work. I was one write-up away from being fired. So I packed some clothes and books and climbed inside his U-Haul with his two dogs and my silver spray-painted bookshelves.

# 8

"STOP MOVING," HE SAID. The orchid breeder must've painted my pussy seventy times. I shifted in the white lace doily he liked me to wear like a skirt. I kept rubbing my thighs because I had goose bumps. After these modeling sessions—in the cold motel room we were renting by the week—he would drive us around San Francisco in his baby-shit-brown Gremlin with bullet holes in the door while we looked for an apartment. But first, we found his dealer. Fritz was always on the corner of Haight and Fillmore. Fritz and the orchid breeder knew each other from college in Boston where they played in a Hawaiian Frank Sinatra cover band. Fritz was a balding guy with frizzy clownish curls who leaned forward so much it looked like he walked on his tiptoes. We bought two quarter baggies and then looked in the Bay Guardian for an apartment. After we'd been tweaking for two days, we settled on a warehouse space that used to be a Corn Nuts factory. We carried his hard, dusty futon into the one musty room and fucked while his eyes bulged like a goldfish. White, powdered speed filled our days and animated our nights. I lived on a diet of meth, hard, dry oatcakes and oranges. After we'd snort the drugs, we'd soak the baggies in our coffee, have line after line, and fuck; he painted wide strokes of labia, one hand pressed down on me like a stop sign. Then another line for dinner.

In the orchid breeder's paintings, I was a riddling sphinx, my face a box of shadows. His silkscreen paintings were pastel layers of pink and gray outlines of my thighs, face, and hands. They were muted layers around a blurry face and long, masculine fingers. The paintings were terrible, lousy, worse than lousy, but you can't tell your boyfriend his paintings suck. He couldn't capture me because I wasn't there. I'd morphed into something else, tiny shards of fragments: an arrow, a train, watery edges of labia. I took myself away, fragment by fragment, until I was gone.

A couple weeks after we moved into the Corn Nuts factory, we drove his car to the Mojave Desert. He fed me ecstasy on the way there, which meant he had to pull over a couple of times and let me barf. We walked in long shadows, sweaty and glistening, touching but not connecting in the heat.

"You have daddy issues," he stared ahead, angry with me out of the blue.

"Look at all of them," I said. He clammed up. I planned my escape while the dust became bubbles inches in front of my face. I tried to bite them: daddy issues in translucent balloons. "They're flying."

We walked in the shadows of the tall cacti. A stick shifted in the shade, which was actually a rattlesnake. It wiggled like a violent wave and shook its rattle. My knees were liquid. I fell back onto a rock as it curled its way away—the same way Mom collapsed the day Dad left.

We camped in sand. A man shook his gun at us in the middle of the night. "Dad?" I bolted up.

"This is private property," the man yelled.

I followed the orchid breeder back to his car where we slept. The next day, his car wouldn't start. It was over a hundred degrees. While we were stranded in the desert, his two dogs ran away. Soon after that, I ran away, too. I found a dinky basement apartment where I wouldn't have to share my speed.

# 9

EXODUS WAS THE ONLY lesbian sex club in town, and my crotch tingled with the possibility of sex with a woman. I walked through the Mission in San Francisco in giant Olive Oyl platform shoes and leopard-print faux-fur shorts. Black halter. Bright red lipstick. Sometimes, I wore a less glamorous outfit: ripped jeans, wife beaters, and Oxblood Doc Martens. Fake eyelashes thick as furs and old lace slips ratted to shreds, but I was anti-glam grunge, a faded Xerox of the drag queens sashaying in my midst. I was on my way to score meth when I met Bianca.

Bianca looked at me. She wasn't an artsy film student who had an accident with a bottle of Manic Panic. She was a dapper girl-boy: tall and lean with fine brown hair and skin the color of Colorado snow. Her sad brown eyes pulled me home when I curled around her. "Ennui" was tattooed in Courier font on her freckled bicep. She tasted like Mountain Dew and was dressed like a forties gentleman in a light green vintage button up shirt and navy suspenders. Men's shoes. Men's socks. Sly smile. I contemplated suicide when she left my side to move quarter baggies around town. Not because I was worried she'd get busted for dealing, but because she was a flirt and I was a jealous bitch. I wanted the speed to melt us into drippy lesbian porridge. I fantasized about living with her in a log cabin near a river where she'd smoke a pipe in a rocking chair and I'd wear fifties frocks and learn to knit. We'd slow dance to Etta James in the kitchen with the smell of sweet potato pie baking.

That's not what happened.

I still posed naked for live drawing classes at the Mission Cultural Center, where I wrapped myself around a chain from the ceiling for hours, sweating for a bump on my ten-minute breaks. "You have a reputation for being late," I was told by pissed off instructors. They handed over my cash and never hired me again.

I always got lost on the way to gigs, except when I rushed to Guerrero Street, back to Bianca. The sharp edge of longing scratched my brain while I drove the wrong way down a one-way street. I couldn't make rent and I didn't give a shit.

But I always found Bianca.

We bought our product from the same clan of fashionable bald fags on Sixteenth Street. They kept the drag queens supplied. Bianca served the lesbians. She also played guitar and sang like Kristin Hersh. She walked into the room and my leg bounced nonstop. I got love spasms. I'd dated women, but this was deeper than sex. This was fucking speed sex.

In our dealer's apartment, she swaggered all cool breezes with a copy of J. D. Salinger's *Nine Stories* in her back pocket. I sat in a zebra print chair with the *Angry Women* anthology and two hairless cats. They wiggled their tails in my face like eels. I was having a love affair with ideas about women and power and sex, ideas Bianca and our dealer had introduced me to. We talked about it like something that was borrowed from a phallic legacy. Woman was a set of symptoms, an "other" to man. The woman in front of me was making me tingle.

I bedded Cixous and her affirmation of hysteria: an inherently revolutionary hiccup in the binary logic of conformity and Christian law. I got behind her agenda to break up continuities and responded to intolerable emergencies with hysteria. I fell for a feminism that encompassed biotechnics and platform Mary Janes, all facets of technology, with a keen interest in exploring the things so many of us in San Francisco wanted to explore at that time: artifice, Baudrillard's simulacra, Donna Haraway's cyborgs, and vintage lingerie. I wanted to tear the woman inside me down and rebuild. I wanted to fuck Bianca.

bell hooks seduced me with her language of rage. She shirked victimization and exposed the American Dream in her raw, angry poetry. Terror was the buy message. There was a war on art, drugs, queers, desire, and HIV.

There was a war on femininity, a war on feminine sex, and a war on queer sex. The feminism I desired called for a remapping of all of my relationships, the disruption of all officially charted maps. It called into question the possibility of love and lit the match of my lesbian body.

In a moment of clarity, I enrolled at Mills College to do a B.A. in Women's Studies. I would better myself; create a new self and a future worth aspiring to. It would take two years and more dollars than I could dream of earning, but time and money mattered little in the battle against the Patriarchy. The problem was that the moment of clarity was exactly that, a moment. My lesbian body was disintegrating up a long plastic straw along with my septum.

Bianca and I breathed in the cat piss and bleach smell of meth cooking in the tiny apartment. The fumes were glorious. We barely spoke. There were fresh fat lines to snort instead. We communicated in seismic waves: two phone rings meant "meet me in the parking garage." We stood there in the amber light and snorted thick chalky shards off glass paperweights and made out on the hood of her Karmann Ghia. We watched the faded sun slip through the windows from the concrete floor. In her garage, we left each other Post-it notes and mixed tapes.

"It's easy to love the beautiful," she wrote. "Love people when they're ugly."

I became monstrous. Hysterical. Beyond the law. I rode the jagged edge between destruction and redemption. I was anorexic and a speed freak and a homeless bum and a strolling hostess and a bisexual dyke addict.

Has anything changed? Does anything change? Could I?

Bianca and I hauled wooden chairs around town and repainted them ten times and reupholstered pillows with stolen fabric swatches. Sharing meth with Bianca was like swimming underwater and spitting lava into her mouth. We held the night up by our arms as the hours collected lint in our pockets; black swollen pupils big as walnuts, locked in a trance. Everyone else fell away like burnt sun.

Speed made me crafty with a staple gun. Falling and flying became the same thing. Bianca was my parachute. There was nothing accidental about it. We rose and crashed. One day became three. I had chronic diarrhea. I cut class, rarely made it to a lecture. Friday became Wednesday; thirty pounds less showed bones in my chest. This was not the humorous, ironic, joyous feminism I'd chased. It wasn't Lacan's jouissance. This wasn't Foucault. This was a living death, memory loss, hair loss. I forgot school, forgot work, forgot home. Forgot you. Forgot myself.

"People should pay you to hang out with you," my dealer said. He meant I should try stripping, but I didn't get that yet. I heard he'd spot me free shit for looking good in his white fur chair. My mom's worried voice on my answering machine became my only thread to the outside world. "You're killing me. Cut up my credit

card or I'll never speak to you again." Erase. Erase.
I was supposed to use her credit card for emergencies
only. I had been using it to bankroll my habit. Habit—it
was more than that, it was life itself. In a négligée and
platform PVC boots, I walked the projects in the Mission
at 4:00 A.M., looking for Bianca.

"I'm really quitting this time," I said. Bianca snorted
a line off a CD cover and one huge tear fell from her
frozen black eyes. I heard Mom's voice on my answering
machine.

"I'm coming next week," she said.

MOM FOUND ME IN my filthy apartment. She looked at me
like I'd become ugly. I was skeletal.

"I have to leave for a while," I said.

"If you go, I'm gone, that's it," Mom said.

"Just for a while." I needed a bump. The voices were
louder. I'd have to cut off my ear.

"I won't be back. Ever," she said. I popped a couple
Xanax. In the mirror, I saw her red nose, her gray marble
eyes. When her mouth moved, I heard:

*Take her by the neck and cut her throat.* I scanned
the room for knives. I kept them under my haunted
television.

"Here's your credit card." I handed her the plastic
pieces.

Would she kill me over this?

"You have to pay me back. This was not a gift."

I'd moved my knives. I checked under the bed.

"I have to go out for a little while," I said.

In response, I heard *Kill her. Snap her neck.* She wouldn't say that. I needed more speed. I needed more Xanax. She was an orange circle, a toothy goblin.

"Just for a while," I said.

In the mirror, my skull protruded. Cheekbones. Rib cage. Pointy nose. Collar bone. Same blue gray eyes as hers. Twin frozen marbles.

Thin at last.

I pulled on a long, soft white T-shirt, crawled into bed with her and waited. She put her arm around my mid section and said, "You should eat." Then she turned on the reading light on her side and reached for her paperback. She had goosebumps on her forearms. I did too, but I was used to being chilly from staying up for days and nights. She smelled faintly of White Shoulders perfume.

"Tomorrow," I said. The walls were getting fuzzier by the second. I was crashing.

"Are you cold, Mom?" I asked. I reached for the burgundy blanket at the foot of the bed and unfolded it; I made sure it covered her legs and smiled at her.

"You're going to lose your teeth. You had such nice teeth."

I leaned my face into the side of her pillow and slept hard.

# 10

"YOU CAN'T BE A bald stripper," Claire said.

"Why not?" I rubbed my newly fuzzy head. My hair was short and blonde. Bianca painted the walls of our apartment seven times and finally settled on battleship gray with burgundy trim. I decided to buzz my hair off.

I wanted to feel the rain on my scalp. I wanted to look like Sinead O'Connor.

"Put this on," she said. She handed me her curly brown wig that smelled like it had been held captive in a bucket of Downy fabric softener since 1985.

"How does stripping work?" I asked.

Staple guns and fabric swatches covered the floor from our reupholstering frenzy that morning. Now Bianca was repairing the dryer. I thought about Claire and her girlfriend working together. They did girl-girl shows at strip clubs in the Tenderloin and made good dough.

"Can I just walk in and audition?" I asked her.

"You should come work at New Century," Claire said.

I offered her a free line of crystal on a glass block, like I did for most of Bianca's customers who were also friends.

"Do they touch you onstage?" I asked. Claire snorted the thin, white line then thumbed through Bianca's tower of CDs. I handed her Rickie Lee Jones' version of "Rebel Rebel" and Sinead O'Connor's "Stretched on Your Grave" extended remix.

"Something more upbeat." She handed me the Breeders CD. Pointed to "Cannonball."

"What do I wear?" I asked. I heard scratching inside a wall. I pulled back curtains and there were construction workers digging a hole in the ground with a jackhammer. I pulled out my entire underwear drawer and emptied it onto the bed. I grabbed a vintage white veil, held it in place on my head, and marched around the room. Maybe I'd pull a string of pearls out of my pussy. I thought of it as performance art, after all.

"Here." She pulled a striped, soft, ankle length T-shirt dress out of a vintage bowling bag, tossed me some scuffed plastic heels and a pair of tight, spandex black shorts. Shadows moved across the streaked walls. "You need a g-string underneath," she said.

I tore through the pile of panties and fished out a black one.

"Take it off on your last song," she said, matter of fact.

I pulled on the baggy, unflattering dress and the too-big shoes and slunk over to Bianca who looked up for a sec then disappeared into her toolbox. Claire nodded. I peeled it off and shoved it in my backpack with a ripped pink lace slip then I poured two long, thin white lines from a Ziploc and offered her a straw. "Lady lines," I said. She snorted it and cringed. A single fat tear fell from her eye. "What if I don't get hired?" I asked. I snorted my line and sniffed hard, then swallowed bitterness. Numb all over.

"They'll hire you. They need girls."

On the bus with my three CDs, and my scraggly wig, the tick-tick-tick sound of mice echoed behind me.

I studied Camille Paglia's *Sexual Personae* and embraced her shock tactics. I'd rebel against male desire and straight attractiveness. Yet, I was going to make my body available to men. Sure, I'd dance, convince them to part with their money, then laugh all the way to the bank. In queer circles, stripping was the solution to the rent problem.

That was the plan before I knew anything about golden handcuffs or hustling, when stripping was art. *Making three or four hundred bucks in five hours would give me plenty of time to study for my midterm exams. Of course I should strip.* I needed rent, and I was getting bored hanging around the house all day with sketchy tweekers camping out in our room, singing Throwing Muses songs. Still, the thought of it made me so nervous I wanted to throw up—which was no reason not to try it.

# 11

*N*EW CENTURY THEATER WAS no theater. It was a cobwebbed dive on the corner of O'Farrell and Larkin Street, next to the famous Mitchell Brothers club. New Century was the Mitchell Brothers' skanky stepchild. I was anxious about the audition, so I walked to the corner store for gum. A tranny in a wheelchair was bumming change out front while smoking a Pall Mall. "Nice wig," she said. I dropped a couple quarters in her Styrofoam cup. She glared at me. "You idiot. That's my coffee."

I scurried through the entrance to New Century and stared at the posters in the windows featuring stars with boobs the size of watermelons. No way would they want my barely B-cups. My hands trembled. "Can I audition today?" I asked the man behind the counter. He told me his name was Manny and handed me a job application form to fill out. New Century was a dark, musty theater with metal seats facing an enormous stage and a long, dramatic catwalk with poles on both sides of the stage. The air reminded me of old mattresses and Lysol.

"Go upstairs. I'll come get you for stage," Manny said.

I walked up some steep, narrow stairs into an attic with a low ceiling and gray metal lockers. I put my bag down on a chair and got undressed. I secured my frizzy wig and attached my faded white wedding veil. I peered into the big cracked mirror and smeared on bright pink lipstick.

Downstairs, two identical twins were onstage dressed in black PVC dresses with ringlets that dripped down their backs. They were gliding across the stage to the Pixies' "I Bleed." Their creamy skin glowed illustrious under the lights, their dresses fell down to the black stage, and their eyes were locked together in an embrace. One unfastened the other's bra. They were mesmerizing. I would have to do something extreme to get hired—I was clunky and out of shape. I had stage fright. I felt dizzy and clumsy.

When my turn came, I was blinded by the lights as "Cannonball" by the Breeders started. I jerked and moved too fast but couldn't stop. Speed bubbled inside me, and my jaw ached from grinding my teeth. I slipped into some cheerleader moves, but tripped. Claire's shoes were too big. I held the pole and noticed goose bumps on my arms. It was freezing out here. At the end of the song I pulled my slip off, tore the straps free then walked backstage. I fastened my wedding veil in place and crawled back onstage, punctuating the drama of Sinead O'Connor's goth remix. I flung my bra into the darkness—towards the only man I could see. I aimed for his glasses, which reflected the stage lights. The song was ending, so I grabbed the pole and hoisted myself up to stand, pulled off my wig-veil and tossed it onto the stage in front of the man. I slid onto my belly and lay face down with my arms straight out in front. I figured the glasses man in the immaculate white shirt would give me my first lucky lap dance.

I felt proud—I'd reached the end of my first routine. I walked offstage thinking, *This is something I could get used to. It might be something I could excel at. This could work...*

"Don't ever do that again," Manny said, wagging his finger at the wig in my hand.

"Do what?" My heart was about to explode on his shiny brown shoes.

"And, dance more slow."

"Oh. Sorry." I fastened the wig back on my head.

Being scolded wasn't part of my feminist manifesto.

"You want to work here, you have to work day shift," he said. He paused like he was expecting me to decline his offer.

"Okay, I will. Thanks." I smiled widely and gave him a thumbs up and walked into the dressing room where there was a white board with names written on it like "Violet" and "Luscious." Manny looked at me, a sharpie in his hand.

"Well?"

He exhaled a great, impatient sigh. "I don't have all day, princess," he said.

"Camille?" I blurted out. After Bianca's Karmann Ghia and Camille Paglia. I immediately regretted it. Camille sounded like lavender-scented baby wipes or tampons. I wanted my name to be "Blue" or "Roxanne" or something ballsy and artsy but it was too late. For now, I was stuck with "Camille." Maybe that name would psychically transport my girlfriend into the musty New Century theater so I wouldn't have to be there alone.

Manny walked down the creaky stairs and back to his perch behind the front counter. I sat at the dressing room mirror with busty girls who were applying face powder with expertise under dark yellow lighting. I felt shabby and greasy. I was jonesing for more speed, too. I didn't match up, not in comparison to the women around me. They paid top dollar for their costumes. This was a joke, right? We weren't supposed to dress like the girls in *Penthouse*. We were playing with artifice and identity, no? We were revolutionaries fucking with the artifice of representation and having a face-off with the phallic transmission system. The artifice was on our side, right? I crumpled in the mirror, afraid of my image. My pupils were dime-sized, eclipsing the blue. Dark brown shadows collected underneath my eyes. I hadn't slept in three days. The sound of hyper rats scraping along the ceiling kept distracting me as custard-skinned girls glued on eyelashes and curled their hair with necks like tipsy swans.

Mom kept calling. I kept deleting her voice mails, but I always listened to them. I always listened to the whole thing. "Where are you? Where's my girl? I've been trying to reach you. Call me when you hear this. Call me."

I SECURED THE WIG with bobby pins and walked downstairs from the dressing room into the audience to watch and learn. I was paranoid. My skin was cold and jittery, and I heard girls whispering. I stood around, maybe for an hour. I was a failure—way too flat-chested for this job. The women around me were soft and languid and knew the lingo. I was brittle and stiff. A blonde girl in white smacked her gum right beside me.

"What do you say to them to get them to get a dance?" I finally asked.

"Ask them if they wanna play with the kitty," she said and blew a bubble, staring straight ahead. She had pink barrettes and white knee socks. Her name was Madeline, and she kept ordering pizzas from the pay phone, but the pizzas never showed up. Her nappy dealer boyfriend did. He sat in the audience waiting for her with his arms folded across his chest. She sat next to him for a long time. I counted five songs that she stared into space. They didn't look at each other. Then he split. When I saw her later in the dressing room, her skin was gray and dead.

Onstage, a woman danced with long red braids and a tiny waist. She was at least six feet five in heels.

"I don't know if I can do this. I'm in love with my girlfriend," I said to Madeline. She bumped against my hip with hers and laughed. "Don't make a fuss, just get on the bus." She giggled and drifted away like a phantom Barbie.

I did more meth.

IT DIDN'T TAKE LONG. The touch of strange hands crawled across my thighs, ass, and breasts, and my first instinct was to swat them away. Soon, revulsion became compliance and compliance turned into assertive hustler. I enjoyed the power I had to turn men on with a gesture, a look, a phrase. I kept my feelings at bay in order to do my job.

It's not that I made killer money right away. I rarely left New Century with over two hundred bucks, but it was enough to keep my speed habit fed and wine bottles around the apartment, at least for a while. I could walk into New Century whenever and leave whenever, as long as I did my stage shows and paid the stage fees. I could wear black lacy kinder whore costumes. This other thing I became, "Camille," was not a stretch.

Stripping was another rush I came to need. Not that I had other skills. I drifted from lap to lap and collected cash from men who became devoted customers. I watched and learned from girls like Danielle Willis. She was skinny and pale and long from her nose to her fingernails. Sharp knife hip bones jutting out of her expensive Victoria Secret lace bra and panty sets. She floated across the room in buckle boots, a fishnet shirt, and not much else; she danced to Siouxsie; whispered things to the men, and to me, while bent in half. She ensnared them; she secured regulars. I learned by watching her.

She was just so fucking sexy.

Camille was this other thing, who smiled when she was sad, and grinned even bigger when she was angry, and laughed when she was rejected. As Camille, I tried to maintain my militant feminist ideals within the context of lap dancing. I tried to feel empowered while swatting men's fingers away, and I always came home with cash to Bianca. But often what I really felt was mangled, by the way the system rewarded me financially for disregarding my boundaries. I broke my own rules, crossed my own lines of conduct. Survival took over in the cavernous frenzy of the clubs as wallets opened and closed. I told myself men weren't invited into my life or my skin, and then began to have orgasms during lap dances—which did feel like power, for two minutes.

I allowed myself to get off so I could focus on work. I'd find a man who wanted me and gyrate on him like a piece of furniture until I came. I never shared my orgasm with them. It was only for me. I felt distraught that I'd morphed into a caricature, ignited by men's desire for me. I became that thing for that cash, and the line that once separated the dancer from the girl reduced to a fine spray as the system had its way.

# 12

TIME WAS A HURRICANE with Bianca: weeks and months of snorting and fucking; more former than latter. Then silence. She ignored me so I stripped more, moved on to a bigger and better strip club called Crazy Horse. We stopped talking. We grew chilly from the speed and from the neglect that happens when two people love each other plenty but love their drugs more.

When I wasn't at Crazy Horse, I worked part-time at a used clothing store, Wasteland, sorting clothes and arranging shoes with all the local punks. Marya swaggered in one day to shop for a belt buckle. She was the Rhinestone Cowboy of dykes with black leather motorcycle pants, steel horns pierced through her chin, and spurs on the heels of her black boots. She passed me her number on a torn piece of binder paper, which I wrote on the beam upstairs in the break room with a black sharpie. I called her on my lunch break.

"What are you doing later?" she asked. My heart flopped out of my rib cage and onto the floor, begging for water.

"Not much."

"When are you off work?"

"I live with my girlfriend," I said.

The next day, she came into Wasteland again. She brought me a six-dollar burrito and a huge orange soda in a white cup. I crossed and uncrossed my legs in a plastic chair that wobbled and made a farting sound when I shifted. We made each other laugh, and I realized it had been months since I had been touched by someone who wasn't paying me.

"I'm one year sober," she said with one hand on my knee. "I'm going to a meeting on Capp Street at ten o'clock. You could come." I was snorting a quarter of speed every couple days. I'd soak the baggie in my morning coffee to get out of the house and on the train to the Haight.

AFTER WORK, I WALKED to the empty apartment Bianca and I shared, uncorked a bottle of red wine that was on the kitchen counter, and took a swig. I found a ripped red and black slip and put it on with fishnets and platform boots. Then I walked across town to the AA meeting where I knew Marya would be. The AA meeting was in a tiny, bleak, dark room. Marya glowed under an old, dusty fringed lamp. The coffee tasted like dead water but I drank it anyway, listening to addicts complain about their rent being raised. I sank into a stained couch that smelled like pee. Winos and hookers wandered in from the dim streetlights and doorways, looking for cookies and shelter from the relentless night. The guy reading from a white paper said that anyone who had consumed a drink or drug in the last twenty-four hours should not share but just listen. I bristled with anger and guilt.

Marya tapped me on the shoulder.

"I'm sending a driver to pick you up from Crazy Horse—Friday at seven." She put her arm around my neck and looked down my slip.

"I can't. You should leave me alone," I said, jutting my nipples out at her. Bianca and I chose meth over sex. Marya woke up something else, something that scared me. I went home and snorted a fat line of speed, praying it would save me like a God.

Friday at Crazy Horse, I piled my costumes into my locker and faked a headache when Marya's truck showed up with the hazards on out front. I got into the truck. "Hi," I said. The girl who was not Marya drove in silence with a smirk on her face until we got to the top of a hill, across from a park where gay men sucked each other off in the bushes. She parked and opened my door and pointed towards tiny cement steps leading down to a basement apartment.

Marya opened the door and nodded to the chick then she grabbed my arm, tugged me inside, and slammed the door. She held a long knife to my face. I wished she would. "This is what you're gonna get if you say anything but yes," she said. Her grin was greedy.

She pushed me towards the black leather sling in the middle of the living room. She flogged me for a long time with a leather paddle, then fucked me with a huge black silicone cock while choking me. It was so much better than doing meth and listening to Joni Mitchell with Bianca.

"You're mine now, " she said.

Hours later, I took a taxi back to work at Crazy Horse, covered in bruises and hickeys, bloated from the maple sugar candy Marya had fed me. I made my usual lap dancing dough, which I brought home to Bianca.

"I made a mistake," I said.

Bianca's eyes were closed. Her stomach was concave and her hip bones poked out of my favorite flannel plaid boxers. It was rare to see her sleep. She was still and quiet. She had been up for three nights, swallowed a couple Zanny's, and crashed hard for twenty-four hours. Her breath was shallow and slow. She was my favorite Bianca when crashing. "I slept with someone else," I said. I rolled over beside her and faced her.

"You slept with what?" She shot up and leapt across the room. She wouldn't look at me.

"She came into my work. I slept with her." A fat line, the burn down my throat, to get gone. I wanted to fall inside her and fill the space between us with speed. I wanted to fix her, fix us.

"I want to stop. I'm going to AA," I said.

"You're one of them now." She was right. I was one of them. An addict, a coward, and an AA clone quitter. On top of that, I was a cheater.

I knew how to stop all this. I grabbed a serrated knife from the drawer and held it in the air. She looked at the knife, and then me, and cried "no, no," in a nasal voice that seemed to come from the next room. I held it up. The knife was something we could agree on. I hurled it at my left wrist. I didn't feel the cut at first, but I knew it was there. I collapsed to the floor slowly on my knees. I felt dizzy, light-headed relief and there wasn't pain exactly, just a floating. I stared longingly at a bottle of Jameson. I heard The Pixies CD on shuffle and imagined dancing in PVC buckle boots. My limbs buzzed. The knife was bloody and must have dropped from my hand because it was on the floor, too. Blood squirted onto the yellow tiles. My right hand drifted over to my left to cover it up like a piece of paper over a random turd. Bianca tied my wrist together with a faded blue bandanna that she had around her forehead earlier. I watched her lips say, "Don't look down. You'll freak out." But I saw the inside of my arm, the veins and tendons and deep red river, paused, not flowing.

The voices stopped.

# 13

"THAT WAS CLOSE." A man in scrubs leaned over me. His head was brown and fuzzy and he smelled like cinnamon. I wondered what this snickerdoodle was talking about, and then I saw black hairy stitches crawling across my wrist. "Were you trying to kill yourself, Miss Crane?" He asked.

"Umm," I said. It felt like a war in my stomach. I recognized something I hadn't felt in a while: hunger. I craved donuts.

"Was this a suicide attempt?"

"Where's Bianca?"

"Do you have a relative we can contact?"

I thought about Mom. I thought about her phone calls. I thought about the last time we had spoken, how proud she was "to have her daughter back."

"When you come visit, you won't believe these tomatoes," she'd said. She was right. I couldn't believe the tomatoes. I wanted to camp out in her greenhouse and tug her tomatoes off the vine and squirt seeds all over my white shirt and taste the sweet juice. "Chris finished the barn last month," she'd said. She had two horses so far, boarded by neighbors. She fed them apples from her tree every day. I couldn't have them call her. I couldn't disappoint her like that. Especially now that she had horses.

I said, "I wanted to feel...different." A chubby nurse arrived and told me to sit down in a wheelchair. She pushed me through the corridors into an elevator and across a pathway to another part of Davies Medical Center.

"Are we going to get something to eat?" I asked her.

"They'll answer your questions at intake," she said. A weary couple was watching Oprah in the waiting room. I wondered if I was being held prisoner. I wanted to go home but realized in that moment that I couldn't, not to Bianca's house, not with the mountain of meth on her desk. I could go to Wasteland and find a co-worker to crash with. I woke up to my name being called and walked up to the little window.

"Down the hall, second door on the right. Knock on Dr. Beemer's office."

I smelled meat and heard furious laughter. I hoped for food: pancakes, muffins, fruit.

A PUFFY, TAN GUY wearing all white with a long, scraggly beard and silence beads around his neck answered the office door. There was a Bob Marley poster behind him. He was dressed in all white.

"Have a seat." I sat down. There was no way in hell this hippie had food for me. There was a rose quartz heart on his desk. Sandalwood incense burned. I wrinkled my nose.

"What's going on at home?"

"Nothing. I got in a fight."

"With a serrated knife?" He fingered a rubber ball and laughed softly.

"I didn't want to die. I just wanted to feel something else." There were several books on chakras on a shelf.

"Hold this crystal. When you feel angry—have you tried yoga?" I took the rock. It was cold and slick. I wondered how many dirty fingers had caressed it.

"When can I go home, Dr. Beemer?"

"You want to go home?"

"Yeah. I want to eat. And sleep."

"That's a good place to start. In seventy two hours, you can go home."

I didn't go home to Bianca. I crashed on a friend's couch and borrowed her clothes. I was petrified to be alone. Even though I wanted to, I knew I could never go back to that speed hut. I could never see Bianca again. I didn't trust myself, and I knew I'd never be the same.

# Part 3

*"Looks like fun."*

# 14

*I*NSIDE THE LUSTY LADY, a baby-faced punk boy with a blue Mohawk sat at the front desk and sketched with a black pen. I was damp from walking up Kearny street with my heavy bike messenger bag on my back. I placed it at my feet. He looked up when I approached.

"Hey, what's your name again?"

"I don't have one yet." He scanned me. I hoped he wasn't staring at the white plastic hospital wristband, poking out from underneath the leather-studded black cuff where my fresh stitches itched. The phone rang once. He picked it up, still looking at my face. I smiled stiffly. How could I have forgotten to snip off the ID bracelet?

I started to panic. I really needed this job. I'd overstayed my welcome on my friend's couch and needed to scratch some cash together to move in to my own place. Bianca snickered when I told her I'd gotten sober and powder-free, that I was moving on.

"I have to at least try," I said. I owed everyone money. Not forty bucks here and forty there, but hundreds to friends, creditors, the IRS, and the DMV. My driver's license had been suspended.

Word was The Lusty Lady wasn't sleazy, risky, or competitive. The Lusty Lady was where I could dance sober and rebuild myself into a person Mom would be proud of.

But first they had to hire me.

"I have an audition here. Can I send her back?" His voice was cheerful and casual like he worked in a record store. He handed me some papers to fill out and a blue pen. There was nowhere to sit so I leaned on his desk.

"Is it okay to do this here?" I asked.

"Of course," he said and returned to his drawing. The forms were the exact same generic job application I'd filled out to work at cafés and clothing shops, except The Lusty Lady wanted to know my dancing experience instead of my retail experience. When I got to the "who to contact in case of an emergency" line, I hesitated. I hadn't told Mom about the psych ward, the stitches, or my decision to start stripping again sober.

The Bic pen I'd borrowed dangled from my mouth and spittle leaked out. The Mohawk boy saw me wipe it off. "Shannon, the show director, will be up in a sec," he said, like it was a done deal.

I figured he was just being polite to the drooling girl. It was his job. No way would she hire me. I was sweaty, puffy, and out of shape. A tall, big-boned blonde with wavy hair appeared from the snaky, black hallway. She waved a long-sleeve-bloused arm to point to the wall behind me which had at least twenty Polaroids of pretty, well-groomed girls in lingerie with names like "Princess," "Star," and "Cinnamon" sexily posed. "Stand right over there so I can get a picture of you. Then you can audition." I didn't feel remotely sexy or attractive, but Shannon snapped the shutter and out slid a photo that was placed in my employment file.

The new sober weight bulged out of my cheeks and hips. I'd been eating nonstop since my hospital stay at Davies and looked like hell, but I signed the contract anyway, agreeing to work at least three shifts a week. I was so chubby that my first stripper name should have been Donut, but I wrote down Lolita and decided to burn the black tips off my hair with bleach later.

Shannon was peppy with expensive-looking highlights. She pointed to the hallway and said, "The dressing room is up those stairs. Take everything off and get onstage on the next song."

I walked down the dark, narrow hallway carefully dodging the crumpled Kleenex on the ground and opened the red door. In the mirrored room girls stood around naked brushing their hair and reading books. It was a well-mannered vibe, much different than the cigarette smoke, rolled up dollar bills, and tiny booze bottles on the counters of the full contact clubs.

In the strangely tidy dressing room, I froze. I had never stripped sober. The mirrors were clean. The counter tops had boxes of Q-tips and makeup brushes. New curling irons were plugged into outlets—like a spa. *What kind of strip club has clean mirrors and un-scummy carpet?* I reached down to unfasten my brown, flared cords and paused. I felt like I might die from over exposure right there. I didn't have the buffer of speed or the warm, casual compliance of alcohol. I felt wrinkled, puffy, and ashamed of my nudity. I wanted to disappear into one of the silver lockers and slam it shut.

*Forget it, I can't do this.* I didn't know what I was supposed to wear—or not wear—onstage. I had brought a crumpled vintage slip and an old black lace bra. I was holding both when Hole's "Doll Parts" started. Maybe the bra would work. Courtney Love moaned "I am doll eyes," and all I could think was *I'm not doll anything.* I pulled off my pants and shirt, grabbed a white boa that was hanging off a hook, and wrapped it around my neck. I fumbled with my scuffed platforms and climbed the stairs to the stage, a big box surrounded by way too many mirrors. I noticed the other girls were totally nude so I wiggled out of my underwear and tossed them onto the dressing room. I tried to ignore my obvious fear of the mirrors and moseyed to the corner booth where Shannon was watching with her clipboard. I jerked, startled by the chorus of girls singing, "Yeah, they really want you..." then moved my hips in circles in rhythm with their voices.

I heard, "Hey, that's my boa." The sugary voice belonged to Marya's ex-girlfriend, Rhea, whose golden bob and tall, perfect, pizza-whenever skinny bod glistened next to my drab sausage thighs in the mirror. Marya had told me Rhea worked there, but I wasn't expecting to bump into her onstage that day. Rhea was a flirtatious and gorgeous mash-up of Uma Thurman and Renée Zellweger, except smarter, with natural D-cups.

"Oh shit. I'm sorry. I just grabbed it for my audition," I said and then regretted saying anything at all because I had an audience.

She danced over to me and curled her arm around my waist. "My boa looks great on her, right?" She was talking to the dark moustached face in the glass looking back at her like she was an ice cream cone. I followed Rhea. She lifted her svelte leg and said, "This is Hole." For a moment, I forgot all about being nervous and fat. I laughed, lifted a thick thigh, and placed it on the window ledge. She used the pole as leverage to slide up and down and teased the customers while also mocking them and manipulating her beguiling doll parts for me. Rhea was also an artist, whose sculptures of pussies had been shown in art galleries in Santa Rosa. Marya had told me all about her and how they stole down comforters from a shop once and slept in her black van when they were between apartments. The song ended, and I blew her a kiss and walked offstage, elated.

"You're a little thick for us, but you have the moves," Shannon said. I left The Lusty Lady relieved to work someplace with women who seemed stable and clean. Though The Lusty would be far, far from

Stripper Utopia, I'd dance next to beautiful, empowered women like Rhea— smart chicks who could joke around onstage. Men weren't allowed to touch us, so we had more control over our show. I wasn't expected to touch dick, and I could work with my extra sober weight and still make money. There was less urgency because we didn't have to dole out exorbitant, random stage fees. We'd dance shoulder to shoulder, and I'd piece my life back together. I'd get a place. My wrist would heal. I'd stay away from powder—and I meant it this time. I'd call Mom and tell her about the great, clean club where I danced with women who were sane and friendly. I'd tell her it was safe and clean. The San Francisco wind swirled around my legs like a cat as I walked down Kearney to catch the bus.

# 15

"HOW ARE YOU GETTING by, honey?" Mom asked. I hadn't called her since my stunt at the hospital. I could tell she wanted to come visit and see for herself that I was still sober. I could picture her sitting by the phone, thinking about what I'd looked like last time she'd seen me, obsessively cutting her toenails. I hadn't told her about stripping at The Lusty Lady yet.

"I'm dancing at a really safe and clean place," I said.

"Go-go dancing?" She asked.

"Nude dancing. Behind glass."

"Huh," she said. It was the kind of huh that could be disgusted or curious, depending on what facial expression came with it, but I couldn't see her face.

After a long pause, I got my answer. "Is this something you plan to do forever?" I don't know if she felt conviction in her disapproval or if she thought it was one of those things moms are supposed to say.

Regardless, I wanted her to come visit to make sure things were okay between us again.

Mom showed up a couple weeks later, so I brought her to The Lusty so she could check it out, herself. She'd never been to a strip club in her life. I wondered how she would feel there, surrounded by young, naked girls, knowing I wiggled in my birthday suit onstage instead of working a respectable nine to five in an office. She sent me to the liquor store on the corner for rum and coke. I mixed her a drink. She guzzled it.

"Don't worry, Mom. The girls I work with are in college," I said, selling her on the idea.

"Hmm," she said and raised her eyebrows.

The women in my family were not promiscuous show ponies. The women in my family grew vegetables, sold houses, rode horses, knew shorthand, and typed sixty words a minute. They didn't talk about sex. They married the first man who fucked them. They were presidents of women's organizations and chain-smoked cigarettes. They drank rum and coke and got loud and demanding. They snorted when they laughed, held college degrees, were cheerleaders and Valedictorians in high school, had kids by the time they were twenty-five and knew how to shovel dirt, fish, can peaches, and bake rhubarb pie. They had spectacular legs, big noses, and preferred angry men over gentle ones. They collected local pottery, took out the trash, and wore hippie jewelry.

The women in my family were not bisexual strippers with a tendency to cut and an appetite for speed.

MOM AND I LOCKED arms and walked past the blue-haired punk security guard, through the dark skinny hallway to a large corner booth. I chose a booth where the dancers could see us, too, and slid some wrinkled dollar bills into the machine. Mom flashed her Dentyne smile at Star and Decadence who waved their lotioned limbs at us. I mouthed the word "Mom" at them and they gave me a knowing look that meant "We'll keep it tame." I waited for her to be shocked and appalled. I was ready for her quick disapproval—which is why I always hesitated to tell her when I dated girls. She just walked in one day and found me curled around Bianca and later, threw her arms around her and sipped her whiskey rocks. Mom's flexibility with regard to me was special. Others fit into two categories: winners or losers; I somehow skated on the perimeter of her harsh judgment. It was the same with stripping. I didn't want to disappoint her, but I didn't want to lie to her either.

I tried not to stare while Mom watched tall, goth, Decadence grin and play with her nipple ring. Certain things I didn't mention. I didn't tell her about my regular customers in the Private Pleasures Booth down the hall where I gave private dildo shows to guys by request. I didn't tell her about the full contact clubs I'd worked at before, or the S & M relationship I had with my girlfriend, Marya.

Years later, I wouldn't tell her about Rob, who'd drugged me, or the couple who paid my rent in Los Angeles for years. I didn't mention the boob job or tattoos. It's not that she didn't notice any of those things or that they didn't disturb her—they just didn't matter because her love was more vast than that. Her love was not contingent on my activities or hobbies. It was like floating in a maternal galaxy of warm stardust.

Mom's bright blue eyes darted around the mirrored stage. "It's silly," she said, chuckling bit. "And, it looks like fun."

She was right, and she was wrong.

# 16

ROM OUR FISHBOWL, MEN'S faces wobbled and bobbed. Their blurry eyes darted in the darkness as they watched us dance behind the glass. When the money ran out, the black, rickety partitions slid down with a crash. Hot light bounced against the mirrored walls as I slid down the single brass pole one more time before stepping off the main stage.

My knees creaked from bending over in seven-inch stilettos, and my thighs burned from lifting them above my hips and pushing my pussy against the glass.

It was time for my shift in Private Pleasures. Through the satin red curtain was the bright white dressing room where I snatched my backpack out of my metal locker and filled it with dildos, lube, and a thin, black boa. I inhaled cum and bleach as I approached the cage, using a flashlight to guide me to the Private Pleasures booth. I dodged crumpled Kleenex scattered in corners of the hallway, but one caught on my shoe, and I scraped my heel across the floor to free it. The cage was near the front entrance to The Lusty Lady, where the shock of sunlight clobbered me the same way it would walking out of a matinee into daylight. I squinted and unlocked the employee entrance door, hung my turquoise robe on a gold hook, and crawled into the cage where it was always night. It wasn't big enough to stand up, just big enough to wiggle around on all fours on scratchy red carpet.

Inside Private Pleasures, I could speak with customers through a microphone from my side of the wall by pushing a silver button. They could talk too, but they had to feed the cash machine or else the wobbly window fell down, separating us by a thick wooden wall. I sprayed Windex on the windows until they were streak free. I arranged my three little dildos on the ledge from small to large and felt sorry for myself for having such an asshole for a girlfriend.

That morning, Marya and I were sitting in her Pepto-Bismol-pink kitchen drinking tea when she saw me shove the dildos into my backpack for work, which meant I intended to use them for my Private Pleasures gig.

"Why ours?" Marya asked. The steam from her tea wilted her green Mohawk. It slid over to one side.

"I make better tips if I show variety." She lunged for a toasted poppy seed bagel, and her monkey tattoo bulged. She dipped a knife into the gob of fake butter between us. Our knees touched. Our dildo was a thick, bright dong with pin, marbled stripes—almost the same color as her greasy walls. *What kind of person chooses that color for walls?*

"Is it for Herbert?" she sneered.

"No. Herbert's a Morning Missile." Herbert was also known as Zucchini Man. He was slim and brown with luxurious black, wavy hair, and he always wore one silver feather earring that dripped gracefully down his neck. He liked to contort himself like Gumby in a corner booth and balance on his shoulders so he could suck his own dick. After applauding him, we dancers watched him lift a zucchini the size of a body builder's forearm from a plastic bag and lower himself onto it. He showed up at 9:00 A.M., right when The Lusty Lady opened; and the 9:00 A.M. clients were called Morning Missiles. I envied him for knowing exactly what he needed to feel desired and seen. His desire was a pure, direct arrow hitting my bisexual gut as I drifted from boys to women and back.

"Throw it away," Marya said. A collection of poppy seeds gathered in her big teeth. She wanted to keep me to herself—or at least the cocks she fucked me with—but, like the last stick of bubblegum in a pack, I always came back wrinkled and soggy.

"What?" I munched the other half of her bagel.

"I bought it. Toss it."

"I'll replace it." I stood to leave and was halfway down the stairs when cold water soaked the back of my faded Pat Benatar shirt and mangled peonies splattered my platform boots. I turned around. Marya, the mellow, soft butch with deep dimples and bloodshot eyes—a lifeguard at an Elementary school—was shaking with rage. I slammed her front door shut, rattling the stained glass tulips, and vowed to do whatever the fuck I wanted with whomever the fuck I wanted—girlfriend be damned.

In Private Pleasures, I pushed the silver button which signaled to clients "I'm here," but no one was waiting for me. Might as well masturbate. Then again, I could be paid to masturbate. When men watched me do dildo shows in the cage, I felt like I had a purpose.

Just as I pulled the oily cabbage rolls from their white takeout box, I heard the steady click of money being counted by the machine. The red digital display showed twenty-five bucks: my tip was five bucks on the twenty. The curtain lifted and a tall man with a wide forehead and noble nose stood in front of me. He waved delicately.

"Hi handsome. On your lunch break?" I said. The tall man wore a suit and a beige fedora. He stood in front of me but didn't speak. He had a rolling black suitcase next to him. *Must be staying at the Hilton*, I thought. He removed his clothes with care like Mister Rogers. He hung his pressed shirt on a fancy wooden hanger and placed it on the door handle. He got naked except for the hat. I could see his busy fingertips moving in the dark. He held scissors and a couple of large black garbage bags that he lifted out of his suitcase, and he began to cut the bags until he had one big flat piece of plastic. He taped the flat pieces together with tape and attached the whole thing to the wall behind him, like a tarp.

He bent over again then popped up holding an enema bag. He held it close to the window and dangled it like infomercial ladies do with porcelain kittens. I placed my hands on my cheeks with feigned surprise. The red digital clock buzzed, alerting the end of our time and the window slid down with its raspy crash. "Oh no," I said. I heard an elbow smacking the door and the rustle of legs hit the wall. He put more money in and the window rose. Our eyes were glued together again.

He showed me that his enema bag was filled with water and he held it up with chalky white gloves. He placed his water bottle down onto the floor. I smiled politely at him. He smiled back with the same smile he gave his five-year-old son on mornings when he'd slice a ripe banana and toss it on top of his Rice Krispies. The same smile he gave his wife after a kiss on the forehead— the same smile I gave Marya that morning.

He inserted the enema bag into his behind and began pumping in the water. I could tell that he was getting full because his expression changed from thrilled to relieved to nirvana, then he cringed. "Oh my!" I said, trying to sound repulsed instead of delighted. I leaned back onto my elbows to watch him from my cramped glass box, cold and slim as a coffin. I opened my chilly legs and turned my rug-burned knees towards him. His eyes were closed. From the cage, my only requirement was to watch him—but I doubted my every gesture. I reached for the lube, wet my fingers with it, and moved them towards my pussy.

"Do you want me to play with myself?"

He shrugged his shoulders.

His expression moved to bliss again, and his forehead bumped against the glass. He vibrated and jerked with peppy violence—as if he were a dancing vessel to be filled up and emptied. His hat tipped and fell off, and his left hand held his cock. He bit the trial size packet of lube with his teeth and set it down on the ledge in front of us. I placed my palm on the glass for a half second, but he kept pulling away from the window—stretching the membrane between us.

Moments later, he came with his hand on his cock and his eyes to the ceiling, water and shit sprayed behind him—raining all over his tarp. He reached into his luggage for a roll of paper towels and wiped his ass. He threw the garbage bags into the trash can and cleaned his hands and legs with antibacterial wipes. He zipped his slacks, buttoned his shirt, and put on his coat and hat. He opened the door and knocked on my window with his clean knuckles. Then he walked towards the pure and silent sunlight.

# 17

A TINY RED LIGHT GLOWED like a Jawa eyeball in the blackness of the one-way booth in the corner.

"Look at that. What is that?" I asked Star.

Dancing next to Star was like dancing next to an Amazonian Bond girl with magnificent natural boobs and a beautiful face. She had soft freckles and full lips, and ornate silver hoops twinkled from her earlobes. She was a belly dancing, fire eating, vegan, bisexual, world traveler. Star was one of many well-read, punk, bohemian dancers at The Lusty Lady, most of whom held college degrees and carried on non-monagamous relationships. Star walked over to the one-way booth towards the red light, where a special thick glass enabled customers the privacy of watching us while we couldn't see them. "You're being filmed," she said to me. "Move over there." She pointed to the other side of the stage. I drifted over to the other regular windows where two men in clown masks and noses bounced up and down wildly jerking off, oblivious to the confrontation happening onstage.

The music mostly drowned out our voices so Star was practically yelling, "I see you." She blocked the window with her whole body. "Turn your camera off. I see you." She put her elbows on the window to block his view. "Turn it off or we will have you thrown out." She spun around and stomped offstage. I bent over for the clown guys who laughed and jerked, their wiry, frizzy wig hair moving in sync, bouncing in the air above them. A door slammed shut. The clowns left. "What happened?" I asked Star. She stood with one six-inch platform heel in a window ledge and moved her pale hips side to side.

"I told her guys are sneaking in cameras and filming us. They could do anything with that footage," she said. Some girls who danced at The Lusty Lady peepshow had kids, teaching jobs, or partners who didn't know they worked here.

"What did she say?"

"She goes, Star, you need to understand if you're uncomfortable, then you can go work somewhere else."

"Fuck," I said.

"And I go: We are all uncomfortable with it. And, you need to know, I'm going to change things around here," she says this to her reflection in the glass where a suit watched her long, strong legs spread for him. The stitches on my wrist had healed, but I still wore a black leather cuff to hide the angry red scar. I had removed the stitches myself with needle-nose pliers and rubbing alcohol the week before. I felt giddy, like something horrible and great was about to happen. I believed Star was going to change things, and I wanted to change things with her.

MANAGEMENT CALLED A STAFF meeting and it was during this meeting when I realized our labor war had begun. We brought up the problem with video cameras being snuck into the one-way booths, and our solution was to replace the one-way mirrors with regular glass. "It's too expensive to replace and customers like the one-ways," they'd countered. They also didn't allow us to confiscate customers' cameras—even though the Mohawk boy did it anyway. The only thing management agreed to do was print out flimsy paper signs from their shitty printer with an image of a video camera crossed out and post them. They wouldn't make any waves, so we felt we had to.

Onstage, we made plans. "All they care about is moving customers through these doors," Star said. I knew it was the truth.

"When I had bronchitis, I couldn't find anyone to cover me and I didn't get my raise," Sybil said. Black girls were allotted fewer shifts and hardly ever worked in the Private Pleasures booth. Busty girls had to find busty dancers to cover their shifts. Black girls had to find other black girls to cover theirs. If we didn't find a girl to cover within our "type," we would be missing from the schedule the following week as punishment. In response, we organized. We elected a union organizer and shop stewards. We hired an attorney and got to work. We dressed up in skimpy outfits and passed out free condoms in baskets on Market Street holding up signs that said "Support Your Local Stripper." Our community buzzed with the delight of making change happen, but we showed up to work churning with anxiety. If show directors caught us talking onstage, they would write us up. They fired us for tiny infractions while we researched unions and union busters. Management used every single tactic in the union-busting manual including a poster-sized check for ten grand made out to the union with a sign that said, "Don't write this check," implying that union dues would break the bank, and we'd be better off without the union.

My work place had become a chaotic war zone, but one in which we felt strong and bonded by our determination. We were going to make the world a better place for strippers. We were also scared of the possible repercussions. We taped flyers to the mirrors in the dressing room that said "Bad Girls Like Good Contracts" and left a copy of the book "Confessions of a Union Buster" on the dressing room table. My legs ached from riding my bicycle from the Lower Haight to North Beach in order to avoid being even one minute late, which would get me fired. Velvet whispered to me "watch it. There are moles onstage." Later that day, Summer was fired for talking onstage about the union.

She had a young son and no other job. We walked out in protest and stayed out of the club for forty-eight hours, scared and broke. Our rage only made us fight harder. In the Private Pleasures Booth, I procured support from my regular clients, like Speculum Man. He always brought his favorite dancers toys and kept them at the front desk in Ziplocs with notes. I did a show for him in Private Pleasures and then we made plans to meet up across the street at The Onion where we gathered signatures from clients and friends to support our union, played pool, and talked about wanting our basic rights. During one lockout, Star arranged for one of her devoted clients to do a show with us outside. He wanted to take us to a construction zone where we would cover ourselves in mud. For a day of posing for him in the hot sun we would make a few hundred bucks each. Afterwards, as I cleaned my ears with a pile of Q-tips, I was elated by the feeling of being unified inside and outside of the club. I called Mom.

"Mom, we are trying to unionize at my job."

"The clothing store?"

"No, the place where I took you—the club where I dance. A girl got fired the other day for talking about our union. So we are on a lockout."

"Honey. You don't have to do anything you don't want to do. Remember that."

"Thanks, Mom."

The dispute took months of long negotiations and meetings. They tried to tire us out by protracted delays in order to test us—to see if we really wanted to go through the trouble to unionize. During one of many tedious contract negotiation meetings, we demanded that they rehire Summer. After several months, we won our election 75-15, becoming SEIU Local 790: The Exotic Dancer's Alliance. The Lusty Lady was the first strip club in the United States to successfully unionize. By then, I had already moved over to the full-contact lap dancing clubs to make the real money. But knowing we had won made me dance with a new determination and confidence that I'd never before associated with stripping. I was proud to strip and felt like a member of my community of dancers.

# 18

WHEN MARYA PEED HER pants in front of a judge to get on SSI, I thought it was the most brilliant scam ever. Several of her hot butch friends were doing it. I knew SSI was government support for crazy people, but Marya was totally clean and sober so she couldn't be crazy, or so I thought. She was just enthusiastic. She had gusto. She lived by her own rules, slept until 10 A.M. every day, swam every morning, attended meetings, ate ice cream by the gallon, and was never broke. She prioritized having fun above everything else. This was a huge drag to me because I slaved away at my stupid retail job on Haight Street and was burned out at the end of every shift, especially when I came home from pulling a double shift at The Lusty Lady.

I wanted to be clean and sober, and I wanted to be with Marya. She devoted herself to our sex life like it was a vocation, wanted all of my free time, and nagged when she didn't get it. She didn't like me dancing at The Lusty Lady, and I didn't like her nagging.

She was totally non-monogamous so there were always ex-girlfriends sharing her bed, or fisting parties she had to attend. Marya held fast to what she loved: great sex and magic potions. She discovered new miracle elixirs that she thought were going to cure everything from AIDS to arthritis, back pain, and wrinkles.

The first magic elixir was urine therapy, something she picked up from a compulsive liar at the lesbian bathhouse she cleaned. The woman convinced Marya that the healing properties of drinking her pee would cure her rheumatoid arthritis. Marya followed her advice and swore it helped. Her kitchen always looked like a science lab: pots boiling and large glass bottles full of pancake-sized mushrooms fermenting. I was terrified she'd spike my soup with her pee.

"What's cooking?"

"Kombucha," she said. Kombucha was the second magic potion she became obsessed with. She watched the spongy mushrooms float around in giant jars for days as they got engorged and turned into the fizzy, bitter, brown medicine. She was still drinking her urine, but it wasn't enough. She was still in pain, or claimed to be. I was tired, and growing more tired of her complaining.

"I'm going to have to be in a wheelchair for the dyke march this year," she said, in a depressed voice.

"Really?" I said, impatient and not sure whether to believe her.

She bought a wheelchair, and I avoided her at the march. I dressed up in feathers and glitter and ran around on Pink Saturday with my friends from The Lusty Lady until I dropped from exhaustion. I didn't want to be bogged down by Marya's ailments. She stayed in the wheelchair until she stopped eating ice cream by the gallon, which immediately made her arthritis less severe.

To her, life was a nonstop sex party. Her days revolved around fucking and vacation. She slept with whomever she wanted—sometimes that was me. This was our deal.

"I do whatever I want, but you're my little whore," she said with her favorite knife to my throat. My job was to resist her.

"That's not fair," I said, knowing she'd leave purple welts on my back and ass, like every other time I talked back. I squirmed and moved closer to her.

"How would you feel if Bianca spent the night with me in my bed?"

"You can't be trusted. At least I tell you what I'm doing," she yelled back. Then we fucked for hours and lost another day, missed our AA meeting, missed work, and forgot the world outside.

ARTHRITIS ASIDE, MARYA'S LIFE was charming and mine was shit. I first ended up in AA because I wanted Marya, not because I wanted to quit drugs. I thought getting sober meant living a dull life full of rules, restrictions, and confessions, but Marya made dating just as intoxicating as drugs had once been.

When we had a date I had to decipher instructions and perform them. I wore different outfits in accordance with the characters she created—the details of which I found in messages she would write in chalk on the sidewalk in front of my apartment. I shared the apartment with three other people, so Marya's tactics were public. My three roommates, disgruntled, informed me of the messages scrawled in big blue and red chalk letters by leaving a note asking me to hose off the sidewalk. The neighbors had complained. The sidewalk today, read:

Lulu is an airline stewardess.

Lulu has a shoulder-length red bob.

Lulu chews bubble gum.

Lulu stops by Uncle Timmy's place for dinner after a long flight.

I borrowed a dusty red wig from Cinnamon at The Lusty Lady and chewed bubble gum until my jaw hurt. I brought along a Southwest Airlines duffel bag I'd found in the trash at Wasteland. Marya opened the door holding a wooden spoon and oven mitts. She wore a moustache and had a pillow tucked inside her shirt. The black leather sling was the only thing in its usual place, she had transformed her apartment again: the table and chairs were set for dinner and long, slim, Gothic candles were lit. "Uncle Timmy" spared no expense. "Hi sweetheart. How was your flight?" Uncle Timmy had a lower voice than Marya.

"Looong," I said, and let out an exhausted yawn, like I was weaker than I was, and more vulnerable.

"Come on in and put your things down. I'm making you dinner," Uncle Timmy said. I put my suitcase on the floor and felt Uncle Timmy's eyes on my ass, trying not to break character. In the kitchen, Uncle Timmy was cooking roasted beets and a big pot of vegetable miso soup. Uncle Timmy was insufferable. He kept bumping me on the ass with the oven mitts and laughing till his gut wobbled. At dinner, he spilled miso soup on my shirt, so I had to take it off.

"Maybe you should take your pants off, too," he said and reached under the table with his small hand. He squeezed my thigh.

"Don't touch me. You're not my real Uncle," I pouted. I was dragged to the sling and gagged. That was the first time I felt the pressure of a being fisted, and the tight pressure of needing to pee while Uncle Timmy's hand was in me. His moustache kept slipping off. I felt like my pelvis was being pulled out of my body and my guts would soon follow. The pain was exhilarating the way speed had been. Thankfully, Uncle Timmy used a ton of lube.

AFTER OUR DATE, AS I walked the streets near Duboce Triangle, I saw red chalk hearts with arrows shooting through them and words like "This way to love" on the sidewalk. I figured they were for Marya's other lovers. Each one of them stung. I was jealous, even though we were non-monogamous; I only wanted her. I carried a damp rag with me and wiped out any messages that I found on corners, blurring the words and obscuring the letters.

The next day, when I came home from work, she was waiting for me on my porch.

"I'm going to Italy for a month to hang out with a friend," she said, moving a twig across the sidewalk in front of us.

"What friend?" I asked, my stomach muscles tightening, annoyed at the twig, the sidewalk, and her evasive glance.

"Her name's Critter. I used to sleep with her but I don't know if we're going to fuck, but probably not," she said to the twig, which meant that, of course, they were absolutely going to fuck and prance around Italy together while I worked at my two lame jobs and obsessed about who else was sharing her bed. "But I will write to you everyday and let you know," she said. As if being told she was fucking a girl named after a rat would feel better than not being told. I preferred her lies, but I couldn't tell her that. I clammed up. Jealousy was not invited to the non-monogamy racket. I was failing Marya.

"Letters take a long time," I said. "Hang on." I walked into my apartment and filled a pot with hot soapy water to rinse her chalk instructions off the sidewalk. When I came back outside, both she and the twig were gone.

WEEKS LATER, A BREAK up letter from Italy said goodbye in three languages, as if we hadn't already said it a thousand times before.

# 19

WITHOUT MARYA AROUND, I attached myself to Jessa, my AA sponsor. When my mouth watered at the sight of powder—like when Taylor asked me for a dollar bill that she then rolled up tight and snorted a line off the counter inches in front of me—I clenched my teeth and went back to putting on makeup and curling my hair. Then I slammed my locker shut, rushed upstairs, and got busy making between three and six hundred untaxed bucks in about four hours.

The Market Street Cinema was the filthiest strip club in town, with old televisions suspended in the air in the audience where porn played nonstop on a gray static loop. In the audience, dances were twenty bucks, but in the back area, in closed off horse stalls, men could get a forty dollar topless dance. Bent nails stuck out so we had to walk carefully or get scratched and need a tetanus shot. At the MSC many of the girls had pimps, like Pandora, who popped in from hooking on Capp Street when she cleaned up. When Pandora was spotted in the dressing room, we would clutch our Hello Kitty purses extra tight and be sure to lock up our costumes while we danced onstage because we would be robbed in seconds.

The MSC offered full contact lap dances, which meant hands all over my body, in the crevices and cracks, breath on my neck, my ass in their hands, an occasional tequila-scented tongue in my ear, and being face to face. In the audience, we stayed in our bikinis for lap dances that lasted a song long. Guys could touch us all over on the surface, but they weren't allowed to put fingers inside of us. Behind the curtains in the back, it was a constant negotiation of hands, money, and antibacterial baby wipes. A nude dance lasted about three and a half minutes. The buzz of making piles of money kept me awake until 4:00 A.M. most nights, but it was never enough. I wanted more. Dancing and performing was exhilarating. I loved choosing a three-song set that matched my mood. Still, as the money poured through my hands, I spent it faster than I could make it. I burned through the cash until my bank account was overdrawn and then raced back into the club to make more. I knew there was more to life than this (tailoring my personality and body to appeal to the men paying me while I was squandering my time in the bowels of the MSC ), I just didn't know what to do about it.

I had followed Jessa to the MSC because she was my idol. She had told me that the real money was in the lap dance clubs, and she was right. Within a few weeks, I had stacked up enough dough to pay all of my tickets at the DMV, the utility bill that was in my name, and all of the friends I owed money to. I was fascinated by Jessa's ability to dance sober. She looked like a muscular mermaid with blue star tattoos that covered her stomach, thoroughbred thighs, and bright orange hair that swung in thick tresses down her back. She had a quick answer for everything—a clever magnetism that was beyond big boobs and firm abs. I watched her talk to men and their expressions slowly softened; she made them feel complicated and important. "Teach me how to hustle," I said one afternoon as we shoved tuna sashimi in our mouths before our shift at the MSC.

"Remember their name. Remember their dog's name. Compliment them. Ask them personal questions. They want to open up." She made it sound easy. Her customers bought her stereo equipment, clothes, shoes, perfume, and followed her like Jesus' disciples; my customers slid off me and moved onto the next girl. Jessa had staying power. She could convince you to buy her granny's dentures, still soaking in baking soda, and you'd happily glue them in place. "Let's feature," she said. If it was her idea, I was sure it was a good one.

"Can we do that even though we aren't porn stars?"

"Yeah, we just won't be paid by the owners."

"We should call our act 'Pigs on Ice,'" I suggested, since I battled weight gain, and we did synchronized pole tricks that looked like water ballet without the water. We laughed and got busy planning. Jessa hired a choreographer to teach us how to do fake splits, or "stripper splits," where you sink down until your hands catch you and then cross the front leg over the lower one on the floor, moving across the stage. We looked like a couple of crabs in stilettos. I got splinters on my kneecaps. After that, we had to have several meetings to download our music onto a pile of CD sets. "If we are going to do this, we are going to be the best drag queens out there," she said. We had matching outfits made, and recorded elaborate three-song sets for our big debut. In an effort to make the most money in the shortest period of time, we would be the main performers and do four acts per day, pay no stage fee, and work all week from 11 A.M. to 1 A.M., straight through. We would get exhausted and irritable as we hung upside down on the pole in roller skates, grinding our hips to "More Than a Feeling." We stripped twelve hours a day everyday, despite headaches and colds. We argued, then made up. We met guys on unemployment who camped out all day long and watched our shows holding signs that read "We Love Josie and Lolita."

We met a choreographer in her dance studio in the Mission who watched herself in the mirror while we slid across the dusty floor. Our timing was off. Her modern dance moves and ballet posture were difficult to learn. Her neck muscles were long and lean. We never quite got the routine down, but we performed it at the MSC anyway. I got splinters doing the walking splits and we ended up ditching the choreography anyway—it was too fussy and took too long.

We had many three-song sets with a theme, but we were no Porn stars. For the "clean" set we dragged a kiddie pool with water onto the catwalk and extended it from the stage and into the audience. For our dance, we stripped off vintage lace teddies and lowered ourselves into the kiddie pool, pretending to wash each other. We realized our act's humor because we were the clean white girls who wouldn't get our hands dirty, everyone else made money giving handjobs or more. Jessa got so angry that we ditched the clean set after one performance. We worked with a dozen black girls who had names like Versace and Chocolate. They only danced to hip-hop like Lil' Kim and Snoop. They taught me everything I know about hip-hop and rap music and how to move to it. They stood and watched us do our "Pigs on Ice" act with their hands perched on their hips, in turns laughing and yawning.

The harder we worked at our synchronized pole tricks and choreographed sets, the clearer it became that the audience didn't care, but the girls were amused by us.

We didn't make as much money as we had hoped, but we had become the "Pigs on Ice."

In the dressing room mirror, Jessa locked eyes with me and said, "I'm quitting these meds. They're making me fat."

A couple weeks later I got a call. "She took a bunch of pills," Sky said. I walked up Jessa's stairs into her studio apartment. She was sitting on a chair, vomiting on the floor. Jessa was so pretty, even with gray bile on the sides of her mouth. To me, she had everything figured out. She had more discipline and more determination than anyone I'd ever met. It was no wonder guys fell hopelessly in love with her and sent her flowers, stereo equipment, and piles of cash. I looked at her face and saw she was fragile and brilliant and soft. The anger from before bled out and now she wore a slack smile.

"I don't want to give up my sobriety date," she said, after they charcoaled her stomach in the hospital.

"Who said you have to?"

My anger became a knot of fear in my gut as I drove home that night feeling the cool wet air on my nose. Jessa was a God to me. She had kept me sober for five years. The fog was heavy and cold. Without her I felt more alone than ever and stupid for not being able to help her. Back at my apartment, not even Mom's voice could comfort me. "I went to the Farmer's market and bought acorn squash. You wouldn't believe all the kinds there are to choose from. Kinds I've never heard of. Yellow and green and weird shapes. Plump and ripe. You've got to come to the farmer's market when you visit. It's right in old town by Ramone's bakery. We'll go there next time you come. When are you coming home?"

# 20

"THE LOSER MOM LITERALLY opened the car door and ran off while the car was still moving," Mom said over the phone. "Why do women like that have kids?" My brother, Alan, was living out of a van with his two-year-old daughter. He'd been crashing at her place, but, unless he could come up with some cash to buy a trailer that he found, he was about to be homeless again. "He's selling pot," Mom sighed. "At thirty-eight years old."

"Put him on the phone, Mom." I heard her call him from the kitchen and then his voice on the line, "Can you help me out with a few hundred bucks, sis?"

"Yeah, I'll send it to Mom in a couple days," I said. The last thing I wanted to do was work an extra shift at the MSC. I was sick of dancing. I was bored, stuck, and lonely. Alan talked fast. He yammered on about a trailer he'd found that he could park in Mom's driveway until he secured a room to rent. He'd been out of jail almost a year. I was proud of him. The last time he went to jail, a guy died on the property where he was building a fence so he was considered a suspect, and at the time, he'd had a bench warrant. "My life's going to shit," he kept talking about his single-dadhood troubles buying diapers and milk. Even though he had applied for GA, the paperwork took a while to process.

"It will get better," I lied.

At work, I sat in a black chair in the audience waiting for customers to walk through the door. I watched Diana, a sad pinup with red tattoos and a Marilyn Monroe smile, pose to a Sugarcubes song. While she danced, I fantasized about going someplace as far away as possible, a place where I could think. I needed a time-out. I wanted to meditate on a new job, on the possibility of a new job—of a change, of something other than extracting money from men who didn't give a shit about me outside of our two-for-one lap dance. I wanted to sip espresso and keep my bra on. I wanted to jump out of a plane or trek through a jungle—go shopping for a God instead of cha-cha heels. I felt dirty and tired and depleted from the inside out. Strippers expired after a few years. *How long could I keep this up? Did I want to? Would I have to?*

I walked up to a man who smelled expensive. I detected expensive cologne like Tom Ford's Amber and admired his crisp light blue dress shirt. He looked about forty-five with a strong jaw and toned arms. *Three hundred for my brother,* I thought and sat down. He told me about his dot com gig in Silicone Valley and his ex-wife who he still loved and who lived three houses away from him. They even went to bikram yoga together. He told me of his plans to travel to Romania. "Why Romania?" I asked him.

"I'm going to install cell phone towers," he said. We talked some more about motorcycles, relationships, and books. He loved Flannery O'Connor and James A. Michener. He listened to Leonard Cohen and Robert Johnson. I'd found a kindred spirit in the snake pit. He grew cuter by the second.

"I need a change," he said.

"I like you," I said.

"You say that to everyone."

"You haven't paid me enough to lie to you yet," I said. He reached for his glass of coke and chewed on the red straw. He smiled with his whole face.

"My name's Peter," he said.

"Stevie."

"Let's go upstairs to those VIP rooms, Stevie." I felt my head nod like a circus monkey and took his hand in a loose grip. I walked up the carpeted stairs and led him through a beaded curtain.

"Put your weapons on that table," I said. He chuckled.

He removed his phone, lighter, keys, and wallet next to a Venus de Milo lamp. The room had white fluffy clouds painted on the blue walls. Then he plopped down on the sticky, black vinyl couch.

"Before we begin, I want a promise," he said and handed me eighty bucks.

"Sounds serious." I slid my sparkling bikini bottoms to the floor.

"You're going to let me take you on a motorcycle ride to Santa Cruz to my favorite Italian restaurant."

"Tonight?"

"No. Tomorrow." I took his arms and slid his smooth hands over the surface of my chest, belly, and inner thighs. His hands were smoother than I expected. I unbuttoned his shirt and slid my hands inside and over his whole back. My thick hair fell onto his neck.

"Maybe," I said and propped myself onto his lap so my face and boobs eclipsed everything else. My hands reached behind him and swiped the wallet from the table and the next second—I wished I hadn't done that. I had to hurry. I counted his money behind his back as he buried his face in my chest.

"You feel really good," Peter said. He was hard. I was disgusted with myself. I took three crisp twenties from his wallet and swiftly put the wallet back. He was hard.

"You feel good, too." I unzipped his pants and reached inside his boxers to tickle his balls. I put my hand around his cock and squeezed. I undulated with my hips and kept rubbing his cock.

"Do you want to do another song?" I asked.

"How long have you worked here?" Peter removed my hand and held it, then zipped up his pants.

"Too long," I said. I wanted to slip into the red black crack between the vinyl couch and the wall and hide there for the rest of the night.

"Dinner. Tomorrow." He wrote down his number on a book of matches and handed it to me.

"You're sweet," I said.

"We'll leave early, about five," he said. I pictured myself on the back of his Ducati, with my arms clasped around him tight. My defenses melted for a moment and I felt my ribcage swell. I wanted to stop stealing, but not tonight. Not now. I stiffened as soon as he stood up to leave. I hoped Peter would walk out into the wet night and not forget about me in about ten seconds, like the others.

"I'll call you at noon," I said. I pictured him reaching for his wallet to pay the cab driver and noticing that he was missing sixty bucks. He would probably think he spent more on drinks than he'd planned, or that he left some money at home on his desk. He'd think about my tattoos and wide smile and wonder what my real name was. He would wonder if I meant it when I said I would definitely call him because I genuinely liked him. And, although hundreds of men would be wrong to think those things after having a lap dance with me in the VIP area at the MSC, Peter was right.

I called him. I got his answering machine. The man's voice said I'd reached Brian.

# 21

*I* NO LONGER HAD JESSA. I no longer had Marya. And the one person I'd met who I'd actually liked had lied to me about his name after I robbed him. I just couldn't do this anymore.

Everyday I woke up in a panic and searched for job listings under the nonprofit section on Craigslist. I liked the sounds of "Peer Educator" and "Caregiver" but I had no qualifications. "Stripper" was not an occupation to list while seeking employment, even though the customer service skill set was applicable to any straight job.

On one of my strolls to the corner for coffee, taking a break from applying, I met a guy named Tom who resembled a young hippie version of Robin Williams. He was sipping on a latte while reading the *San Francisco Bay Guardian* and told me about a job opening where he was working as a case manager for homeless youth. He jabbered on about how he thought everyone was attracted to him—his boss, his co-workers, and his clients. His boss called me later that day to set up a meeting.

It was pouring rain the day of the job interview. I was so nervous that I asked my friend Jen to give me a ride. In the passenger's seat of her SUV, I broke down.

"Why are you crying?" she asked.

"They're going to know I give handjobs." How do I tell them about the gap in my job history over the last few years?"

"Tell them you were in school," she said.

"Do I look like a hooker?" I asked.

"No. You look like a classical musician. Don't worry about it." She dropped me off in the Tenderloin. The interview lasted over an hour because I was interviewed by two groups of people: the human resources staff and the Polk Inn staff. I picked at my fingernails underneath the table where they questioned me, but not my job history. The thing they were most worried about was my long-term jag in Alcoholics Anonymous.

"This is a harm reduction program so we don't talk about abstinence from drugs or alcohol." Tom hired me, regardless of my career as a lap dancer. It was my first job in years that didn't involve being naked. Every time I showed up for work I was afraid that I was going to be fired for being a hooker in AA. Everyday that I walked through the doors of the Polk Inn and wasn't, I won a tiny victory.

# 22

*T*HE POLK INN STOOD out in the Tenderloin because of all the beige and glass, a contrast to junkies out front selling stolen bicycles and gizmos. Winos waved their lotto tickets in my face brushing past its elegant modern angles. Tranny hookers stopped to check their weaves in the windows as they strutted by. Everyone was holding.

I was hired as an RA, residential assistant, an entry-level counselor position that required no actual counseling, but my duties ran the gamut. I was a nurse, babysitter, DJ, watchdog, secretary, and cook. I distributed meds and dinner for a half-dozen seventeen to twenty-four-year-old HIV-positive, mentally unstable, drug addicted clients. Then, I encouraged them to dispose of their hypodermic needles in bright orange Sharps containers that were attached to the walls. During my shift, I recorded the clients' notable behavior in a big black plastic binder that was kept in a locked drawer upstairs.

For the first couple of months at Polk Inn, I hardly recognized myself—the role, the people, even the small talk. But I grew with it and found myself looking forward to every day. I was helping people who needed it, and that felt good.

Our clients at Polk Inn participated in street economy, meaning most of them turned tricks, hustled drugs, or smoked dope with the ghetto blaster guy who bounced up and down the sidewalk, nodding his head to the rhythm of Coolio's "Gangsta's Paradise" while singing "the ones we hurt are you and me." Polk Street was their terrain. My job as an RA was to enforce the house rules. Clients weren't allowed to bring their swag into Polk Inn and we reserved the right to rifle through their backpacks and purses. I never did. We buzzed clients into the front door and they willingly held out their hands to show the things they carried: a wrinkled brown paper sack from the liquor store full of cigarettes, candy, and beer. My manager said their world was small and that they stayed within a four-block radius of the Polk, but that wasn't all true. Some clients wandered—like Charlie, a gorgeous, blonde, crack-smoking tranny. They had rules and they had chores; they had to keep their rooms clean and show up for their meetings with their case managers in order to remain there.

I sometimes helped write cover letters, or hung around in the reception area handing out sack lunches to clients and making sure they included a turkey sandwich, a Capri Sun, chocolate chip cookies, and a mealy red apple. When the clients were really good, I got to give them a movie pass.

At five, the case managers went home, the fog wiped away the sun, and we RAs took over the Polk Inn.

ARMANDO WAS SHORT AND thin, a five-foot-tall Latino with loose khaki shorts and a studded black belt. He smeared grease on his slick black curls and wore a chunky silver rope chain around his fragile neck that seemed uncharacteristically butch. Armando had been a resident for a few months and was twenty-two.

"He's a cutter," Phil, the other RA, warned me. I'd already liked him. Now, I really wanted to help him.

One afternoon, Armando was sitting in a chair in the courtyard, slumped over a black journal with a set of skinny pens, drawing. Once in a while he wiped a shiny ringlet aside with his right hand, then picked up another pen and shaded.

"Want a snack?" I asked him. He shook his head and tore another piece of coarse white paper from his journal, drawing in loopy, magnificent detail. I looked over his shoulder at his drawing of a giant menacing orchid overtaking an angel wielding a sword.

"That is so good," I said.

"I'm going to the Academy of Art." He stood up, eyeing his work from another angle, then sat back down. His forehead was creased.

"Can you play some music? Phil always plays music."

"Sure." I saw a Radiohead and a Jill Scott CD that another RA left behind; I popped in the Jill Scott.

"Thanks," he said.

I looked forward to my shift on Sundays because I cooked an early dinner and it was movie night. My usual dish was chicken smothered in olive oil and wild rice with almond slivers. A red key dangled by an elastic cord from my wrist. It opened every door in the building, and while I cooked it jangled against the refrigerator and pantry with a loud, tinny clank. I found garlic, butter, and carrots in the fridge. I rifled through the dishwasher for cooking pans. I chopped an onion and tossed chicken and vegetables in the oven. The smell of my cooking helped kill the antiseptic institutional smell of frozen French fries and stale fish sticks. The kitchen had sliding glass doors that opened onto a patio where clients smoked on aluminum chairs in the chilly, afternoon sun. White plastic ashtrays were filled with rainwater, butts afloat in the soot.

*Miss Congeniality* played loudly on the big flat-screened television in the community room—the movie they'd voted for unanimously.

A woman I didn't recognize showed up on the security camera in the front office and rang the bell. She held what appeared to be hundreds of white lilies wrapped in Saran wrap and said they were from a wedding. Could she donate them?

Armando put down his pen and smiled huge.

"Lilies! My favorite!" he said. "Can we decorate?" We spent the next hour cutting the tops off of water bottles and filling them with water from the sink. I unlocked the case managers' offices and Armando pranced into the room, cleared space on each desk, and placed the flowers. Then he sauntered off with jerky dance moves, threw his hands in the air as if to say, "Ta da!"

"Can I have some in my room?" he asked, knowing I would allow it, knowing that I was a pushover. He didn't wait for my permission. I watched him carry two bottles of flowers up to his room on the second floor, right next to the RA office.

I didn't see him for the rest of my shift, until I knocked on his door to give him meds. When I did, he showed me two small, framed pictures of his mother and sister. Their faces were round and hazy like from an eighties after-school special. They hadn't spoken to him since finding out he was a gay hooker. My entry for him read: Armando was social, helpful, and productive. He worked on his beautiful drawings and helped me decorate.

# 23

AT POLK INN THERE was no such thing as a normal shift. There were times that "normal" included all hell breaking loose. I clocked in one Thursday to learn that Allesandra had been killed in a knife fight, out in the street, and Revo had disappeared. Luca had OD'd, and Heather was in the hospital in labor. Sometimes life and death would cozy up beside each other. This all during the same day I was reprimanded for allowing Armando to get anywhere near scissors. "They could cut themselves on the edges of those water bottles," my manager said. He was right, but I didn't feel remorse. I thought it was good for Armando to do something thoughtful, and we shared a love of lilies.

I walked into the kitchen, which is the first thing I do when I need a reset. I stood in the chilly glow of the fridge and considered my options. I swiped a Capri Sun and sucked the wet sugar from the spindly straw. It was eerily quiet under the florescent kitchen lights. Charlie rushed out the front door in a denim miniskirt and spike heels with a little wave. I ordered Domino's pizza in case some clients showed up for dinner. I heard loud music blaring from upstairs. It was Armando's room, so I grabbed his meds from the office and knocked on his door.

"Can you turn that down?" He opened his door a couple inches.

"Why? No one's here."

"I'm trying to order us pizza." His eyes were two black holes.

"I'm not hungry." I handed him his meds. He shook his head then shut the door in my face. I ducked into the RA office and wrote in the binder:

"Armando was asked to turn his music down. Refused his HIV and psych meds."

Downstairs, I gorged on three pieces of drippy pepperoni pizza and replayed the night with the client I'd decided to meet. I was shocked at how easily I'd crossed the line from dancer to hooker. I grasped for excuses but was disgusted with myself. Had the street economy invaded my skin? Why lunge deeper into sex work while trying to distance myself from it?

I used my red key to open an empty client apartment and locked myself in the bathroom. I stuck my finger down my throat and puked. I wanted to sit in the dark and blast music, rock back and forth in my own emptiness. Rock my emptiness to sleep.

Armando's music played louder and louder.

"Goddamn it," I mumbled. I walked down the hall and banged on his door. He didn't open it.

"Armando!" I kept knocking. Louder.

"I'm coming in, Armando." I unlocked his door and, noticing my key chain still had some puke on it, wiped it on my jeans. The door was heavy because he'd used a bookshelf to blockade it. I pushed my whole body against it, sliding the bookshelf towards the wall. Armando stood holding a wooden bat in his arms. His head was cut and blood dripped down into his perfectly tweezed black eyebrows. Blood was splattered on his hands and shirt. His eyes were fierce and lacked any of the softness from the day we'd arranged the lilies. His gaze was ecstatic and free, like an angel floating in cool moonlight.

"I'm okay," he said.

He let the bloody bat drop, and it landed with a thunk. Both of us froze, standing in the dark room with his blood under our feet. White lilies drooped pitifully on a wooden bedside table. My manager had confiscated the water bottle.

"I'm okay," he said again in a raspy whisper. We glowed in the dark. I backed away, stepped into the hall, and called my manager. Armando's door slammed shut.

"Call nine-one-one," my manager said. I didn't want to. I didn't want Armando to go anywhere. I wanted to throw a blanket over him and pat him on the head and hand him a sack lunch and a movie pass. Within a few moments that could've been thirty seconds or a half-hour, the door buzzed.

Outside, the ghetto blaster guy was still swaying to rap music. Behind him were six men in black helmets and kneepads. I'd never seen them before: the SWAT team. They wrapped Armando up and carried him away on a stretcher. His expression seemed to ask me, *Why?*

# 24

RED PAST-DUE NOTICES PILED up as my bills went unpaid. I was behind on rent and had exhausted my list of people to touch for a loan. So it wasn't long—in fact it was soon—before I was back moonlighting in the Tenderloin clubs, trying to make some dough, to get my head above water, to breathe. I reasoned with myself, told myself that I was adding something to my clients' lives in both places. Or at least that I wasn't causing them more harm. I told myself that I catered to the needs of somewhat helpless people. Call it denial, call it a girl making a living, or trying to. I hadn't completely separated myself from sex work, and I was used to the sexual validation. Without it, I didn't know myself. I wondered what it would take to disentangle, to totally leave sex work behind.

A few weeks after Armando cut himself, I rode my motorcycle a couple blocks up to O'Farrell on the wet cold night where I was stripping at New Century Theater till 4:00 A.M.

New Century was empty except for a few coked up firemen. They weren't supposed to be there, but everyone knew they bought their powders from Carla. They did blow in the bathroom and leaned against the walls of the club. Sometimes I'd talk to one of them, but I couldn't waste too much time flirting—I needed money to pour, not trickle, in. When the DJ called my name to dance onstage I was about to give up and go home. "I'm leaving after this set," I told him as my first song by Danzig started. A tall, fat guy in a suit and tie walked up to the stage with a pink drink in one hand and a twenty spot in the other. He threw it onstage and staggered away. I removed my bikini top and tossed it onto the floor. After my third song, I walked over to him and his friends.

"All dressed up and nowhere to go," I said.

"I wouldn't call that dressed up," he said pointing to his lap. I sat down there, and his friends roared.

"I'm Stevie," I said. My lips touched his ear lobe. The music was so loud I felt the bass vibrate my tailbone.

"Do you want to make some money tonight or what?" He flashed a tennis ball-sized chunk of hundreds—enough to pay my rent, buy groceries, gas, maybe some new lingerie. "I'm Rob," he said, then told me he was one of the founders of one of the biggest magazines in the country. I talked him into a dance, and the suits egged him on with high fives. He took my hand and they patted him on the back—universal reactions when a guy agrees to a dance, at least in any club I ever worked in. Rob followed me down a glowing hallway that led to a private room with an Egyptian theme, paintings of scarabs and pyramids reminded me of lost civilizations and strong women like Nefertiti and Cleopatra. I was sweaty from my stage show. I sat down on the black vinyl couch seat. My thighs stuck to it. The song started so I draped over him in slow motion. "I've been looking for someone to pay," he said.

"Well, luckily, I showed up for work today," I said. He handed me two hundred dollars and gave me a card with his phone number and email address.

"I mean, outside of here," he said.

*Oh shit,* I thought. This would mean more than a handjob. This would mean crossing another line. I was supposed to be stronger than that. I was supposed to be a role model. My managers at the Polk Inn would call this "acting out."

That was a lot of money, I reasoned. I could just meet Rob for dinner. Lots of girls met regulars outside of the club. I gave him my number.

"I know a great place for dinner. Call me." When he called, a couple of days later, I'd already forgotten about him.

"Do you like sushi?" he asked.

"Love it," I said.

"What kind of music do you listen to?" he asked.

"PJ Harvey, Tricky. Nick Cave," I offered. Was this an invitation for a rock concert or a blowjob? I started to wish I hadn't given him my phone number. *I've never met a client for dinner. Why am I going to now?* The silence was sticky and my right hand was trembling as I turned on the stove to heat water in my red teapot.

"They have terrific tuna tartare at Asia de Cuba. Meet me there Friday at six," he said. I hoped he didn't think this was a freebie. Guys always think dancers will date them for free. I'll talk to a guy in the club for a half hour and suddenly I'm their girlfriend. Sometimes they'll send flowers to the club with notes like, "Don't forget to call me, Stevie."

"What time?" I said.

"Will you do full service?" he asked. I was quiet for a moment in my red kitchen with its silky blue curtains. The silver teakettle I purchased at a junk shop in the Mission whistled. My black and white tile floor was dusty. I wiped a drop of goop, probably honey, off the floor with a sponge. *What was the question again? Right. Would I fuck him for money? It would be more than I was making in the club and it would take less time. Should I be talking about this on the phone? Was he a cop?*

"Okay," I said. I poured hot water into my favorite red mug, watched the bergamot tea bag steam, and felt the warmth of it on my face. "Yeah." Just like that.

"How much?" he asked.

Start high, I thought.

"A thousand, I guess," I said, taking a stab in the dark.

"I was hoping for eight hundred, but I won't haggle with you."

If dinner was a hundred fifty bucks, eight seemed fair.

"Okay, eight," I said and wondered if I would be expected to do oral. *If so, for how long? How many positions would be expected for eight hundred dollars and whom could I ask?* No one. I was too ashamed to ask anyone. *Would he have condoms?*

THE NIGHT I MET Rob for our eight hundred dollar date, I had been hanging out at my new AA sponsor's house in Noe Valley. I missed Jessa, who I hadn't heard from since she swallowed a bunch of pills and took off to Morocco. I wondered how she was doing and worried about her, too. I even prayed a couple of times. When I mentioned stripping to my new sponsor, she tightened her hands around a mug of coffee, slid it closer to her chest and said, "You owe all of the wives and girlfriends amends for helping their men cheat." I didn't mention my plans to meet Rob. I was going from stripper to hooker without much hesitation, and my secret scratched at my insides during the cab ride towards the hotel.

It was a cold San Francisco night, and the fog unraveled like a soft ribbon over prim Victorian homes. Inside the lobby, there was a giant fireplace and a hot pink chair that looked like a prop from the set of *Alice in Wonderland*. There were digital interactive portraits on the walls that blinked and changed expressions when you looked at them for more than a half-second. I recognized Rob at the bar. He was sipping an orange cocktail and pointed to a glass of water in front of him. "This is for you." I gave him a we-are-not-total-strangers kiss and sat down beside him on a wooden stool.

"We're on a waiting list for a table," he said and glanced at an expensive watch. I didn't know what to wear for a paid date. There's no brochure to consult. I didn't want to look cheap, so I chose a coffee brown top that hugged my cleavage and black cigarette pants. I should have worn a dress, gone for a more professional appeal. I regretted carrying my big bottle of water into the hotel. I set it on the floor.

"You look sweet," Rob said. Three pretty girls stood nearby in skirts scrolling through their cell phones. I reminded myself that I wanted one.

A few sips of sparkling water later, my head started to float above my body, and I felt warm and syrupy. The glass in my hand tipped sideways, spilling some water on the bar. I laughed and reached for napkins. "What did you tip that bartender?" I said. I moved off the stool and grabbed the bar. The music pulsed, and I shivered from a sudden chill. The bartender was at the other end with his back to me, talking to a girl in a black tube dress.

Rob's grin became long rabbit teeth encased in wax. His lips were wet with words that made no sense. Conversations garbled around me, and the music circled my face like smoke. I thought about yelling, but no sound came out. The girls chatting nearby turned into mannequin-goblins.

"I want to make you do things," Rob said. His words came from land, but I was underwater. His eyes were white glossy eggs. There was a terrible cackle.

"Bathroom. Be right back," I said. The digital portraits mocked me all the way to the lobby. My legs went rubber, and my feet were full of helium. The scenery blurred: fuzzy, swimming bodies in a Roadrunner cartoon. I found the restroom and lunged towards the mirror. My pupils pulsed from small to large like they had acquired a heartbeat in my absence.

My head was intact. I touched my neck to make sure, then placed my palms on the cold walls. In the mirror, my cheeks drooped.

In the mirror, I whispered, "You will eat. You will act normal. You will take his money. When this is over, you will buy a cell phone."

I walked back to the bar where Rob waited.

"Hey, cutie. Our table's ready."

"Great," I said. *Motherfucker*, I thought.

The waiter pulled my chair out, and I sank down. I flirted and giggled on cue and asked Rob, "Is that Polo by Ralph Lauren you're wearing?" I devoured crab cakes and quesadillas and lettuce leaves doused in citrus oil. "You've got a great appetite down here. I hope you do upstairs," he said. The waiter appeared with ice water in a dainty glass.

"Can I have a large bottle of carbonated water instead?" I decided the waiter and I had a telepathic understanding. I winked at him. He knew what was happening and was waiting for my signal to call the cops. Undercover vice would arrive and haul Rob off in handcuffs. He would be the one trapped. The waiter and I would instantly fall in love and would leave this hotel and decorate our flat with hot pink love seats and ivory curtain sets from Bed Bath & Beyond.

We skipped dessert, and Rob paid the bill. He led me into an elevator. It stopped at the eleventh floor, but no one noticed us, and no cops came.

In his suite, everything was virginal: white comforter, white curtains, white walls and candles. I watched him undress. Rob was pushing three hundred pounds. In more svelte years he'd been a football player. Rolls of fat spilled out of his waist now: years of tacos and crème brûlée at the executive desk of his fashionable magazine empire. He unbuttoned his shirt with thick fingers. I smelled pork and garlic. He was a powerful man. I thought of my AA sponsor. *Which lie did Rob tell his wife? Was he in Chicago giving a talk or at the gym with his trainer?* He took stiff bills from his wallet and placed them under a metal lamp, then laid down on the white bed.

"Join me?"

I took off my clothes and climbed on top of him. We were in golden candlelight, and the quiet room was dim and holy. I used my teeth to rip open a condom and studied it. I found his cock under soft flesh and slid the condom in place. His smile was greasy, and the room smelled like jasmine. I felt numb, as if he was fucking a postcard of my pussy. The white sheets got wrinkled and he finished.

I stood up, took the money and my clothes, and walked into the bathroom, a small box with sharp white angles. I counted eight hundred bucks and threw up in the toilet, coughing to hide the sound. I wiped my mouth and slipped the bills into my jacket pocket. I tore the ribbon from the tiny soap and washed my hands with lavender suds. I got dressed then waved goodbye from the door. He was snoring.

Outside, heavy mist dropped onto my bare shoulders. I hailed cab after cab until finally one stopped. I rolled down the window and inhaled the cold air, letting the cold wind smack my face. I was ashamed. I'd have to change my sobriety date if I told my sponsor. I watched two men in front of a liquor store carrying someone strapped to a gurney. I dug my fingernails into my thigh until they left a set of white, crescent moon marks.

# 25

FTER THE INCIDENT WITH Armando, I was amazed that my manager gave me permission to take the clients on an outing to Muir Woods. We traveled across the Golden Gate Bridge in the company van one clear sunny day to breathe in the fresh forest air. The mood was good, the bus alive with laughter, a few clients performed party pieces—one sang a song, another recited a poem, they told jokes and even played Charades, as much as as they could while buckled in. None of these people were interested in the other me. Dances, handjobs, and tricks were not on the agenda, and the clubs were a million miles away—I was determined for us all to have a memorable day. We did.

I PANICKED, RUNNING AROUND the place like a mad woman, screaming their names. I'd round up a couple of them and go look for more, come back to the bus, and the first ones would be gone again. Finally I locked them into the bus one by one, from which they shouted names out the windows and pointed me this way and that, adding to the general confusion. It took two and a half hours to round them all up.

I drove back to Larkin Street a lighter shade of green than that morning. It was quiet in the back, where they sat with their unopened sack lunches on their laps.

I was livid again, still livid, but at myself, always at myself, for not having hacked my way to an alternative existence, for not having the guts, for not having the luck. *I'll go back to school and finish my degree*, I thought. *That'll be my ticket out. Has to be. Will it be my ticket out?* I knew strippers with degrees. Hell, I knew one stripper with a Ph D. *It will be different for me*, I thought, *a one-way ticket.*

The problem—well, problem number one—was that I owed Mills College seven thousand, eight hundred bucks from years earlier when I'd dropped out of school to pursue my meth habit. I spend money like a wino on payday. I'm organically irresponsible and impulsive, and stripper money had a different texture. It slipped through my hands like sugar. I spent it faster than I made it. My work ethic lacked luster. I'd wait until I was flat broke to go into work because I liked the desperate pressure of hustling. The more afraid I was, the faster I hustled. Sink or Swim. I knew I couldn't save money on my own and I needed help. I called an accountant friend, Megan.

"Can I hire you to help me save money?" I asked her.

For the next year, Megan showed up at every club I worked about 1:00 A.M. to collect a stack of dough, about three hundred bucks, that she invested into a mutual fund I didn't have access to. Within a year, I'd saved more than enough cash to pay the Mills bill. I even went back and graduated, but the more I wanted to build a life that didn't involve handjobs or stripping, the more alluring was the pull to do exactly that.

Mom left so many voicemails. They all said the same thing: "I'm so proud of you, that you're finally doing something that makes a difference. Call me when you can."

# Part 4

*"Ba-na-na yellow."*

# 26

WO YEARS PASSED LIKE this, living somewhere between stripper and social worker, when I met Ian.

Ian was an olive-skinned, tattooed hairdresser who worked at the beauty salon where I'd made an appointment to get hair extensions. I figured he was queer—like everyone else who worked there—so, when he asked me out, I laughed in his face and went back to my magazine. I figured one of the girls had put him up to it. He came back again, caught my eye in the mirror and said, "Seriously, what do you say?" Offers weren't exactly pouring in. The only men I spoke to were customers in the strip club and clients at the Polk Inn. In my mind, men weren't for dating, they were for money. Boys were drug addicts for whom I doled out HIV and psych meds. If I wasn't dating anyone at all, male or female, didn't that make me simply available?—*Okay, why not?* I thought.

"Sure," I mumbled while Sparrow tugged at my tangled weave.

It was just dinner. And dinner didn't hurt, much, though I spent most of it with my arms crossed, wondering what the hell I was doing. I'd forgotten how to begin with a guy. When he dropped me off where my motorcycle was parked outside his house, I got flustered when he leaned across and kissed me. He didn't have the over-cologned, under showered customer smell. He had ample soft lips and smooth skin that smelled like donuts and weed. I jerked back, afraid I'd be repulsed, afraid I would throw up in his lap, but that's not what happened. The kiss lingered through several Massive Attack and Radiohead songs on a mixed CD. Cars honked and were forced to weave around us. I hadn't enjoyed a kiss this much in a very long time, maybe ever.

Ian was smart and poetic in a way that made perfect sense to me. He played the harmonica and wrote lyrics about smoking and pot saving the world from corporate greed.

"Do you want to come upstairs and see my shoe collection?" he asked.

I followed him upstairs to his room where he kept his bong and we fucked until I was sore and it was morning. Six months later he was my boyfriend, a year after that I moved in with him. On one of those days, I realized I was falling in love.

Then one day, on the way out the house, Ian just announced, "I'm moving to L.A. with my band."

Hating L.A. was in my Northern California DNA. We even had a burl plaque that hung on our living room wall that read, "We Don't Give a Damn How it's Done in L.A."

"You go there, it's without me," I said. He grabbed his black bike messenger bag and hoisted the strap across his chest. Smoothed out his black Dickies.

"Move into the band house with us," he said. I pictured moving into a communal hippie house with dirty floors and full ashtrays; the smell of stale bong soaking into my clothes; nonstop rap music. "L.A. wouldn't be bad for you."

"No way."

He shook his head, gave me a limp hug, and walked out my front door.

Maybe he was right. Maybe I could find another nonprofit organization to work for and never strip again.

We broke up when he moved, but it didn't stick. I didn't know how to stay broken up, especially from Ian, so I gave my two weeks at the Polk Inn and decided I'd find another halfway house to work for. L.A. was teaming with them. I packed up my two bedroom Victorian apartment on Folsom Street, shoved everything into a U-Haul, and drove off to L.A. He moved out of the band house and we hunted for an apartment together.

Our dinky shitbox was right off Sunset, walking distance from a cathouse called Paris Nudes that I hoped I could stay away from. Our apartment building was neon green and had a concrete balcony where Ian kept his bong. It had a view of our parking lot. I woke up to the sound of Russian immigrant senior citizens hocking loogies out the window. If I looked out I could catch a spit tail freefalling like a sparkler, landing on my motorcycle. When I saw them in the street they glared at me like I was smoking crack with their Babushka. I turned away, afraid they'd spit at me if I stared too long.

I'd come to L.A. hoping to quit dancing and start fresh. I missed my old life, the quick access to cash, and the feeling of being desired. Without it, I felt ugly, useless, and numb. I'd been stripping so long, it had become innate.

I dreamed about stripping: I was in a stadium in front of thousands of men, like at a Mötley Crüe concert. Instead of the band playing, there I was, topless. Swinging from poles that reached the stars. I came to, angry and full of dread. I didn't belong in L.A. I missed stripping.

My chubby thighs stuck together in the demonic August heat. I pestered everyone I knew in an effort to find a job that wasn't stripping, but none of my leads returned my calls. It was weeks before I landed a job cleaning houses, cash in hand, but it wasn't enough. I'd have to find something else, learn something new. I was persistent, open to anything. I hoped I could reinvent myself overnight but, even though I had a degree from Mills College and some solid direct service counseling under my belt, I couldn't shake the feeling that I was nothing but a thirty-something ex-stripper with no kids and no husband, desperate for a gig.

The motorcycle couldn't always get me to the houses I cleaned—though occasional, it does rain in L.A.—so I parked it in the garage and bought a bullethole-ridden, crap brown 1978 Disco Nova from a guy named Clyde at Rent-A-Wreck for three hundred bucks. I'd heard about a job in the valley testing porn stars for HIV, but I had to learn to draw blood to do it, so I signed up for the required course. A skinny blonde taught me how to tie a tourniquet and locate veins. It wasn't stripping but it was still working with sex workers. I studied plasma, platelets, and cells. I administered the HIV tests that allowed porn stars to stay on the payroll—in this job I could keep helping people and be surrounded by sex workers without needing to be naked. At least it wasn't Paris Nudes.

I NAMED MY CRAP brown nova Cricket, for the clicking noise. Her AM radio played two radio stations: Christian talk shows and oldies, so I chose Frank Sinatra. When that faded, I listened to murmurs about sin and redemption on the fifty-minute drive from Hollywood to the HIV clinic. The sun baked my arms by 8:00 A.M., so I arrived wilted and sweaty in maroon scrubs. I made small talk with clients while I searched their forearms for juicy veins; spun their purplish blood and siphoned their piss while they told me about their kids, spouses, and upcoming scenes.

Phlebotomy was supposed to be my transitional career out of the sex industry, but it became my gateway back in.

Ian hit his bong each morning and sold pot out of a yellow seventies Tupperware container he kept in our closet. When he was asleep I snagged five dollar bills from that container for gas or lunch money. We were scary broke. He cut hair twice a week and had band practice three nights per week. While he was at band practice, I collected our change and poured it into the machine at Vons that made a sound like slot machines in Vegas. It spat out a coupon for money that I used to buy four-dollar turkey meat I stretched into meatballs in an effort to make it last. I would squirt ketchup into the leftover meat to make spaghetti sauce. Once, a famous drummer I had a crush on raised his eyebrow at me as my change clanked through the machine at Vons. I'd forgotten what it was like to be this broke. I glared at him the way my Russian neighbors glared at me.

At an interview for a bartending gig in Beverly Hills, standing in line with about eighty people who'd also seen the post on Craigslist, a guy a hundred years younger than me with fake blue contact lenses asked me about my work history.

"What about the ten-year gap here in your work history?"

"I was a nanny" or "I was in school" or "I lived with a well-off boyfriend," were my answers. One of the porn actors I befriended gave me a list of catering companies that he worked for when he was between movies. The catering company was in San Gabriel.

They didn't ask many questions, they just told me to show up in black pants and a white tuxedo shirt to bartend a wedding. When I wasn't drawing the blood of porn stars, I bartended Bar Mitzvahs, baby showers, birthday parties, and weddings all of which were intrinsically sad to me. I'd settled into a life of crab cakes and chicken skewers and mini cupcakes that I passed around on brown plastic trays. My boss didn't allow us to accept tips directly, so I shoved dollars into my tube socks and counted them in my lap during my drive back to Hollywood.

My radio was often drowned out by the flashing sirens and helicopters that are everywhere in L.A. and especially near my apartment. It felt like there was always something horrible happening in Los Angeles.

First, there were fires. Thousands of acres were swallowed in orange flames that reached the sky, scorched the hills of L.A., and leveled homes. I was hypnotized by the destruction. Children were abducted; men dressed in Santa suits shot ex-wives in the face. Night stalkers and grim sleepers rose to kill again, and abandoned babies were found in trash cans behind Del Taco. People held signs and begged for money near freeway entrances while gang wars raged.

A couple of months later, on the way to bartend a baby shower in San Gabriel, the Nova died on the 210 Freeway. I called Ian.

"I've got to get to work and the car just died."

"Good luck with that," he said, and hung up. Sitting there on the freeway, at that moment I knew that it was over. I would end it before we'd ever really begun—he had done for me what the orchid breeder had. He had helped me escape something—but he couldn't help me do more than that.

# 27

ANCERS ALWAYS WANT TO quit, but we never do. We're ghosts, dragging our chains from club to club. We appear in the window of your cab when you're on the way to a power lunch. You think you recognize the angle of our jaw. We come and go, but we never disappear for good. We dye our hair, get weaves, gain weight, lose it, get breast implants, butt implants, colored contact lenses, and track marks. We get laugh lines and stretch marks and eye-lifts and hide it all with makeup and glitter. Then we change our name from Candy to Taylor and move to another club across town.

The important thing is to remain in perpetual motion—even if it means a constant red rash on my butt from high-friction lap dances. There were a hundred reasons to retire my Lucite heels. There's no glory in stripping at forty, and I was getting very close.

Maybe, I thought, I could avoid razor burn and whiplash and make more money if I just saw one or two clients privately. But I also thought about the adage about alcoholics—how they never should have taken that first drink.

I was asked to do a mobile draw for the HIV clinic, which meant I had to drive to a porn producer's set, deep in the valley, on a street called Zelzah. The Nova chugged and clicked along until I found the address. I rang the doorbell and was greeted by a guy in pajamas and a white T-shirt. He was in his fifties. "She's in there." He pointed to a room where a girl named Bunny sat on a stool, memorizing her lines, naked to her shoes. She looked lazily toxic as she drooped beneath a pink cowboy hat and looked me in the eye while I drew her blood. I'd brought her most recent test so she'd be covered for the day's shoot.

"How many copies do you want?" Her Gucci suede purple boots reminded me of my old life: the dark circles under my eyes from seeing too many 4:00 A.M.s, the fine lines around my lips, the calluses on my heels, corns on the balls of my feet, the lower back pain, the neck ache, the frantic white highs and the sad, dull crashes.

"Hey, do you want to do a job with me Friday? It's for a couple and it pays pretty good." The fucking money. The fast motherfucking money. Rent, paid. Groceries, bought. I felt my neck turn red and warm like being complimented by a hot, random stranger. My heart raced, my body's automatic rush response to doing a show.

"Yeah. I do."

I TOLD IAN I had a catering gig in Simi Valley and brought my bar kit and tuxedo shirt to work at the clinic. I'd tossed out my costumes when I left San Francisco—at the time it felt like a statement, now it just felt dumb. Bunny said she'd bring me something to wear. I figured our show couldn't be much different than the choreographed bachelor parties I'd done in San Francisco with girls I'd worked with in the strip clubs. How different could it be than giving handjobs in the private rooms of the Market Street Cinema? This was my fault. Ian was used to my cash flow. I spent money as if I still had it and resented him for not contributing more. I festered, propelled by frustration. Ian wasn't a man who liked to work, and I was a woman who grew up with eighties-specific optimism that promised success if I worked towards my dreams. Both my parents reinforced their "You've got to get up everyday and hit that ball hard." I rose early and always showed up for class. I believed that higher education guaranteed upward mobility and job security, apple scented hair and expensive jeans. That house in the Hollywood Hills was totally doable as long as I was willing to "wake up with the roosters so I could soar with the eagles."

# 28

BUNNY PULLED UP TO the clinic on Friday at closing time with her liquid smile dripping down at the corners. We headed towards the bathroom to change clothes. Off came the baggy, shabby scrubs and on with the pink g-string and the white, shiny, tiny shorts. On top, a tight white tank top with a plastic heart and patent leather red cha-cha heels.

You never know when you'll need a sharp, spiked heel.

Bunny fastened the shiny black buckle on her baggy red and white Santa suit, complete with red faux fur pom-pom hat. The whole thing stunk of mildew. The top was tight and had two big gold buttons that were bells. The skirt hung loosely on her hips and had a big fuzzy white border along the bottom. She popped a small white pill then slowly applied cherry red lip gloss in the mirror. It occurred to me that our outfits were color coordinated, which put me at ease.

"So what should I call you when we get there?" she asked.

I'd used a million names over the years: Stevie, Rhonda, Violet, Candy, Lolita, Angelique, Alexis...

"How about Rosebud?" She handed me a small white pill.

"I like that," I said, and put the pill in my makeup bag for later or never. I was trying to stay sober—that was something I wasn't giving up on. I clenched my teeth.

Bunny and I carried our things out to her car, which had a bumper sticker that read "Question Reality." I got in on the passenger side next to her Carl's Jr. bags and cans of Diet Coke.

We pulled away from the clinic and drove off into the hot and humid October night and onto the 101 Freeway. Bunny lit a menthol cigarette; she smoked Mores like my mother and squinted her brown eyes. She blew smoke in front of her face.

"So, the wife, Kay, is an ejaculator. It gets all over the place. We eat her out. Use toys on her. Fred mostly just watches."

"It's about the wife?" I asked.

Bunny looked at me and laughed. "No, I wouldn't say that. He won't touch you much. You don't have to touch him. He might kiss you. Depends how high they get," she said between drags.

"How long does this take? An hour?"

I looked at my watch. I was losing a little of myself with each passing moment. I drifted away and stared at the blood orange sun. I thought of the pill I took from Bunny earlier. The pill was oval. Smaller than Vicodin but with an "x" on the top. Maybe it's Ambien. I never favored pills except to sleep after a powders bender.

"A little bit longer." She nodded and fidgeted with something in her purse.

The sun was falling fast and we were still on the freeway, heading North. The more Bunny explained, the more my stomach churned. I looked for an escape, but there was no turning back now. The more nonchalant Bunny was, the more I felt like I was watching a movie of myself.

She said, "Fred might try to shove his tongue down your throat while he jerks off." I pinched my leg. Dug my nail in deep. Maybe the pill was morphine. "Kay will want to diddle us both and squirt in your face."

I chewed my lip. I tasted blood. Her voice sounded like it came from behind us—like there was an answering machine of her voice in the trunk. Klonopin. It could be Klonopin—the king of benzos. She said, "I'm on my period so don't go too crazy down there." I reached for the warm can of Diet Coke from the floor. I couldn't feel the fingers of my right hand.

We pulled up to a white security gate with two burly guys standing in a glass booth. "Bunny for number nine Mustang Lane." They nodded with raised eyebrows but let us through the gate. We continued up a mountain road with cowboy movie street names like Trigger and Gunsmoke. We kept going up and around and two rights and a stop. Generic looking but very recently built mansions were tucked into the desolate canyon; each had the same SUVs parked in their driveway. We got out, and it smelled like horses. She pushed buzzer number nine and another white metal gate lifted.

A graying guy wrapped in a white, terry cloth towel skirt answered the door—the kind with Velcro at the waist for easy access. He said, "Hi Bunny" in a low near whisper but reached for me instead. A sluggish, wet tongue slid into my mouth before I could pull away. He tasted like burnt coffee and blue cheese. His skin was a rough, fuzzy kiwi. He kissed Bunny, too, and we followed him up some wide stairs with white banisters. They led to a dark hallway with brown walls that hinted of smoke.

"How's business, Fred?" Bunny made easy chit chat. Fred was her regular. That's job security for girls like us.

I thought of all the ways I'd tried to get by in Los Angeles. I'd cleaned the houses of swimsuit models, drew blood and siphoned piss, counseled porn stars, bartended baby showers and Bar Mitzvahs, organized storage units and closets. And then there was this. I'd tried to stay away from this. Only when money's tight, I told myself. But money was always tight. I had bills to pay, something I needed, stuff I had to have. I couldn't resist. I could collect a few clients and make more than what my five part-time jobs paid all week. I'd find another topless club with a sorry buffet and slim, gold poles. I'd find more coke dealers, ex-cons, and geezers to dance for; more soldiers with PTSD and government checks—for just enough cash to get me through one more day.

For the first time since moving from San Francisco, I felt hopeful.

"See you two cuties in a couple minutes." He dropped us off in the bathroom and walked down the hallway.

Pot smoke hung in the air like an omen. I heard the clanking of glasses.

*We are in the middle of nowhere and Bunny is the only person who knows I'm here.*

We got things ready. Bunny opened a duffel bag and displayed her impressive collection of dildos: long and black, fleshy pink, swirly purple, and one that was the shape of an arm with a fist; some of them vibrated, and one had a little dolphin on top (it was turquoise), but they smelled like an outhouse on a hot day.

"Jesus Christ, Bunny. Didn't you disinfect these?"

"Sure, usually, but I just came from seeing someone," she said.

"So I smell."

I reached for the faucet in the bathtub and ran hot water, squeezed some orange liquid soap from a plastic bottle and threw the rank dongs into the bubbling brew, angry with myself for not grabbing condoms at the clinic earlier.

"Are you trying to get hepatitis?" I said. I knew better. She rolled her eyes. I heard a knock at the door and Fred's voice: "Girls, are you taking a bath in there or are we going to have some fun?"

I grabbed the black prick and whispered to Bunny. "Clean this one so we can get this over with."

"Take it easy," she said, like I was a buzzkill.

"We're coming!" I cooed. Bunny wrapped a peach towel lovingly around our wet schlong, grabbed some tangerine flavored lube and opened the door.

We were wet with the soapy suds.

"Ho ho ho," Bunny sang at Fred and slipped on the slimy linoleum floor.

"Shit," Fred helped her up and led her down the dark hallway. I guess he was used to this. I followed them into the candlelit room where blonde Kay was waiting, cross-legged, smoking a joint in a tan velvet chair in the corner. Her cheeks sagged with age, but her breasts were two perky plastic oranges in her chest. She wore a Victoria Secret catalogue negligee that wasn't cheap. Her quick smile reminded me just a little of Mom's even grin. She wore open-toed cork seventies wedge shoes and was sipping on white wine. She left a pink lipstick stain on the rim of the glass. She had straight white teeth, whiter than bone.

"Hey cutie pies. Wanna party?" Kay's voice was high and fake. She beckoned us to move closer. She offered us wine from a bottle on a round glass table. "Yeah," Bunny said matter-of-fact. I shook my head. Kay's eyes were like aqua blue birds darting around the room. She was thin, fleshy, not firm. The long blonde hair wasn't hers.

The room was spacious but windowless. It had a fireplace on one wall with some pillows and blankets thrown down in front of it. Dozens of white candles burned, filling the air with a sickening sweet floral cloud. *This will help with our fecal predicament,* I thought. There was a soft California King-sized bed with stuffed animals on top of it. *Were there children around or were these Kay's friends?* Framed pictures on the walls near the fireplace showed an eleven or twelve-year-old girl who looked like she'd had an accident with a can of hairspray.

Fred plopped down on the bed and leaned on his side, watching us. He was tan and maybe sixty. I looked around the room for a clock but the one by the bed was turned around facing the wall, hidden from my view on purpose. Fred's skin was a leathery hide: rough and wrinkled.

A strange porn played on a thin screened television: a woman painted blue licked another woman in full tiger regalia; ears, tail, and black and gold stripes covered her body. They chased each other through a fake jungle then had sex with an orchid. I looked for porn actors I knew from the clinic, but the body paint and costumes made it impossible. Two blondes performed oral sex on each other in a tropical setting. *This must be what Fred expects,* I thought. The sound was muted.

"Make love to her now, " Fred commanded. Bunny crawled on the floor and growled like a tiger. When she was in front of Kay's knees, she lowered her face, head, and Santa hat between her long, tanned, shiny legs. Kay giggled. I removed Kay's négligée and reached for her brownish nipples. They tasted like Jergens lotion. Fred stroked himself beneath the terry cloth towel skirt.

"YEAH. GIRLS. THAT'S IT. That's it," he mumbled. He sped up his jerking animal motion.

After a while, Bunny removed my shorts and g-string and pulled me to the floor over by the fireplace on top of some blankets. I helped Bunny wriggle out of her Santa skirt and panties. Bunny got chatty.

"Your body's creamy and sexy," Bunny told Kay while rubbing her thighs with almond scented oil. Kay's eyes were closed and she was on her back. I took over with the almond oil. Bunny lubed up our long black friend with the tangerine slime and approached Kay's crotch. She let it dangle in the air for Fred to see. Fred had removed his terry cloth number and was rubbing his cock with greasy, calloused hands. He nodded and moaned and I could see cracks in his leather skin in the dim light.

"That's it, baby, relax." He was talking to Kay.

Bunny set down the dildo then licked her fingers and rubbed Kay's clit. She transformed into a gifted fondler before my eyes. Tongue, fingers, tongue, fingers, tongue, fingers and then Kay cried out like a sick cat and squirted all over Bunny's face. My turn. Enter black dildo. Kay started wiggling and moaning and I started to drift, pretending I was watching myself from the wall where the pictures hung. I imagined Kay's pussy as a large hot pepperoni pizza with black olives, mushrooms, and extra cheese. It was a greasy affair, half Canadian bacon and pineapple, sweet, tangy, and hot. It was within reach and I could smell its magic, and I would devour it in a half-second. I bit into my lip while Kay released all over me. Her eyes were closed, and she had soaked the towels beneath her. Bunny's baby voice woke me from the pizza dream.

"Kay looks like a Christmas present tonight, right Fred?" She had fitted the Santa hat onto Kay's head. Kay laughed. I was soaked with foreign fluids; smelling of the ocean, salt water, and almond oil. I wanted to go to the bathroom and wash it off. I wanted to be dry. I wanted to slap Bunny. I wanted to take her white pills.

"I'm ready for a smoke break," Fred announced. He wiped his sticky hands on his towel skirt.

"We're going to the bathroom. Back in a minute," I said and reached for Bunny's hand, motioning to the door. It was time to change toys and find a clock.

One at a time, we washed our faces in the sink. I went for the blue dolphin dildo soaking in the smelly suds in the tub. I waved it in the air above our heads making it dip and dive.

"Let's use Flipper on her," I said.

"I'm not high enough." Bunny tuned me out—sat on the toilet and rested her face in her hands. The clock on the counter had roman numerals. Forty minutes had passed. She took out another white pill and chased it with water she sucked from the faucet. I didn't ask her what the pill was. It seemed too personal a question. I wished time would speed up.

By the time we walked back into the room, Fred
and Kay were passing a joint. Fred giggled and let out
a piggish snort, which made them both laugh hard.
We sank back to the floor, and I presented Flipper to
Kay. She giggled and spread her legs. She wanted me to
massage her thighs and lick her pussy. I wanted to get it
over with and resumed.

Bunny leaned over Kay and kissed her neck, face
and mouth, working her way down to her breasts. Bunny
was like a wind-up sex toy, high and rubbery. An escapist
by nature, I never stay in the room. I float and leave my
husk behind.

Things were going well until Fred decided he wanted
to get closer to us. He rubbed his dark dry skin against
me. It felt like petrified wood. He grabbed my hair and
pulled my head back so hard I let out a little, "hey," but
he ignored me and shoved his tongue down my throat
again. His lips were thin and hard, his raspy voice said,
"Rosebud. Make love to us." I wanted to pull away, but
I didn't. I wanted to ask him about his skin condition.
I wouldn't touch him beneath the terry cloth skirt
because that was never the deal, but he grabbed my wrist
and moved my hand towards it, to test me; to see how I
would respond. I pulled away.

I thought of bolting. I thought of lunging for the
wine glass and hurling it against the fireplace. But where
would I go? A dog howled outside. I could go sit in
the car and wait for her, but then I wouldn't make the
cash. I hated myself for agreeing to do this job and now

there was no turning back, only moving forward. In that moment, I understood how gunmen go on shooting sprees and then kill themselves; and I understood how junkies relapse after many years of sobriety. The only way to squirm out of this was to take the immediate focus off of myself.

"Fred. It's our turn to watch. You and Kay make love now. It turns us on. Please?" Bunny piped up. She was gentle, soft, and non-confrontational. Bunny was the pro. Grateful the world was Bunny's petting zoo, I winked and crawled in her direction.

"That sounds fun. I'd love to see you fuck Kay," I told Fred. Bunny disappeared into the bathroom, I figured she had to pee or pop another pill, and that's when Fred slipped me his number, which I hid under the heel of my red spike-heeled shoe. Bunny emerged later with a clean cotton candy-pink dong that she held up proudly like she'd won it at the County Fair by popping balloons with darts. She aimed to please.

"Ready to play with the kitty?" She grinned rabidly and approached me. Good girl. Pink was my favorite color. I leaned back and licked my lips.

"Let's watch them fuck while we fuck." Kay was tipsy, and her blonde extensions were nappy, wet, and in her face. Bunny plunged pinky inside of me with a blue-collar sensibility: not too rough, but earnest about getting the job done. I didn't mind it, but it was nothing close to sex for me. It was like gyrating on a piece of furniture for an audience's benefit. It's not mutual, just meaningless and numb. I writhed on the floor, then pretended to come violently after a few minutes, which seemed like hours. I even called out Bunny's name. Fred straddled Kay right next to us on the floor and humped her silly, like a dog. She seemed to have the same sort of empty theatrical orgasm that I did, with long, sonorous moans. *Good girl*, I thought.

I sensed the clock ticking. Time is money, and it was time to go. I got up, and Bunny followed me. One shower later and a coat of vanilla flavored lip gloss and we were squeaky clean. We gathered Bunny's dildo collection, and Fred walked us down the miles of stairs. He handed Bunny a wad of money. She handed me half. Four hundred each.

The second we were in her car, Bunny lit a menthol. We were silent on the drive back to the clinic. I felt Fred's number digging into my heel and knew that I'd call him a week later. I reached in my purse for the small white oval pill and felt white chalk. Valium? I rolled down the window, tossed it out, then held my face to the breeze. The smell of horses reminded me of Mom.

# 29

"*J* CAN'T DO THIS ANYMORE," Ian said to the computer screen. I stood in the kitchen, five feet away, washing dishes. We'd been having our Epic Fight. Our electricity was about to be turned off. He didn't care. I did.

"I'm leaving," I said. It slipped out of my mouth, and my feet followed. I walked out of our apartment onto Curson Street in the pissing rain and drove around the block three times. No going back now—a horrible, yet strangely arousing feeling. I sat in the parking lot of Von's grocery store trying to figure out where to go when the phone rang. A friend needed a cat sitter while she did yoga for two weeks in Hawaii.

I asked if I could move some boxes into her apartment, and she said yes. I packed up another U-Haul, filled it with my remaining stuff and Ian's cat, Screech. We both wailed all the way to Silver Lake. Screech took a shit on the rug every time I left for work. It always made me chuckle, a little cat shit seemed a small price to pay for the gift he'd given me. A couple weeks later, she called to tell me she decided to move in with her yoga girlfriend and grandfathered me into the lease. No matter how much I loved someone, I always had to pick up and leave. I have started over a hundred times. Sometimes, that's the most loving act there is.

# 30

*A* FRIEND GOT ME A job working at a law firm answering phones and filing bills, and I kept Fred's number but never called it. I listened to my phone messages on my hour-plus commute while staring at peppy joggers running in the opposite direction towards the reservoir. Mom's voice squealed through the phone, "I got tickets to see Céline Dion!" I despised Céline Dion, but after the breakup, I didn't care what I'd have to endure to see my mom. I wanted to park my car, leap into the pale morning sun, sprint after the joggers, and yell "Mom's coming!" Instead, I rolled down Beverly to Wilshire Boulevard to answer phones for eight hours under fluorescent lights and schedule appointments for Dave Navarro and Pearl Jam.

According to the clock on the microwave, I was ten minutes late by the time I turned on the lights and walked into the office to make coffee. I tore open the individual plastic packets of grounds and tucked a few unopened ones into my purse. As the coffee pot gurgled, I walked over to my desk where there were stacks of client bills to file, depositions to schedule, and a birthday card to sign for one of the attorneys. The little square eyeballs on the phone twinkled with messages, but I didn't check them. I called Mom from my desk. "Fly into Burbank and I'll drive you to Vegas. Let's go together." I sent an email asking for the time off work.

A couple weeks later, I picked Mom up in a rented silver truck and brought her back to my empty apartment. I didn't even have a couch for her to sit on. I took her to Netties, a locally-owned dinner spot near my house. Ordinarily, Mom was sharp and opinionated, but tonight she seemed to drift, lost. On the way to Vegas the next morning, she seemed tense and disoriented. "You are driving too fast" and "I don't remember it being this far away from L.A."

"Yeah. It's just further than I thought."

When we arrived at Harrah's to meet her girlfriends, she got lost in the parking lot and threw her hands in the air, exasperated.

"Where is the entrance?" She yelled.

"Mom, look, it's right down there. See?" I pointed to the escalator.

"How do we get down?" It was a weird thing for her to say. Her world was alphabetized, organized, and meticulous; she was fanatical about paper clips and files.

Something was strange. The air was all wrong. Miss Dion canceled the show last minute, due to bronchitis, so we met up with Mom's girlfriends for dinner instead and played slot machines. Mom wasn't herself. At least, not her usual Mom self. Her skin looked puffy, bloated. Her body had shifted in a way I couldn't decipher. She acted agitated and spaced out.

When I moved a lamp in our hotel room, she screamed at me. "Don't break it!" she yelled and kicked the bathroom door.

"What's gotten into you, Mom?"

"I don't know." She started to cry.

"Why are you so forgetful?" This was our code for Alzheimer's, Mom's biggest fear. Her mother, grandma Ruby, got sick in her early sixties. The thought of losing her sharp mind terrified her.

"I'm not forgetting, I just can't focus." She was quiet on the way back to Burbank airport. I chitchatted about what a shame it was that Céline Dion canceled the show. I made sure she was at the correct airline, then watched her disappear through the sliding glass doors and hoped she would find her way to the right gate.

# 31

A MONTH AFTER VEGAS, MOM turned yellow. Her husband didn't notice. Charlene—the neighbor with the chickens—did. I found out when I checked my answering machine. My car keys still jangled in my palm while I listened to her nasal, small-town twang, chattering about a Thai soup recipe, the peppers she bought at the Farmer's Market, and the co-worker she hated. Then—

"You won't believe this. Charlene says I'm ba-na-na yellow. Anyways, we're driving to UCSF Medical Center for–"

My answering machine cut her off. My keys dropped to the floor.

I called back, but she didn't pick up. It was late so I climbed in my car and sped off to work. In the office kitchen, I watched the coffee pot gurgle, ignoring the ringing phone. I smeared pink lipstick on my lips and pictured my mom's angry liver attacking her golden skin.

*Had her drinking escalated? Was it cirrhosis? Would her liver have to be removed? Could I give her mine?* I checked the mirror for hidden pockets of yellow pallor. I'm my mom's daughter, after all. My skin was hers.

I walked back to my desk, and my manager was waiting for me.

"Can you come in here?" she asked.

I walked through the dark hallway to her cramped office. Billing issue, I figured.

"Close the door." She lifted her Bugs Bunny mug to her mouth, realized it was empty, and set it back down on her desk. Jan's hair was thinning prematurely, causing paralegals to snicker "Here comes the bald eagle" whenever she approached. She was wearing her favorite faded black jeans, which meant it was casual Friday. I glanced at my wrinkled skirt and T-shirt, realizing that I forgot to cover my tattoos and forgot all about casual Friday. She nibbled at a cheese Danish and wiped her mouth.

"I just made fresh coffee," my voice was higher than I expected. Her head wobbled slightly towards the photo she kept on her desk of her husband, a hiker with a beard. He looked ten years younger than Jan.

"So," she said, looking straight at the computer in front of her, "We're letting you go." She shuffled papers on her desk, then opened and closed a drawer. A new shame warmed my neck. Tori Amos must've complained when I forgot to cancel her meeting with her lawyer.

She'd politely flipped through a magazine for a half hour before I noticed my mistake.

Jan swiveled in her chair and sneezed spraying the papers she'd set down in front of me with her spit. It was my employment contract. Panic made me queasy.

"It's at will." Jan sniffled, but it came out like a snort.

"Is it because I'm late?" I asked.

"Your general performance," she said. *Had she read my story on the computer at my desk about my job with the couple?* "We need you to clear out your desk and go." It sounded like a question, but it wasn't.

This was my first real office job. I'd never been officially fired by a management-type person. Strippers don't get fired; we wander off until we come back hungry, full of mangy need. I sent an email to my co-workers, saying goodbye, and slithered out of the office. Then, I hauled ass to the UC San Francisco Medical Center to see about my mom's liver.

I DROVE THE 382 miles on the 5 North, listening to PJ Harvey and pushing ninety most of the way. *There's been a mistake.* My mom was healthier than the horses that had knocked out her teeth when she was eighteen. She told us she had gotten stitches on her bruised and yellow lips, which meant the blood was already rushing to the damaged cells to restore them. Yellow meant healing, right? Yellow was good.

When I arrived at the hospital, she grinned at me and put down her *Woman's Day* magazine. Her face and arms were the color of spaghetti squash, puffy and bloated. She'd ripped recipes and scattered them on her lap like confetti.

"Do the doctors know what's wrong?" I asked her.

My step-dad grumbled, "Too much whiskey in her belly." Disgust was leaking out of him.

"That's not it. See? I'm not shaking." She held her steady hands in the air as proof. She was no alcoholic. Sure, she drank. By age seven, I was making her tea: Lipton with one small teaspoon of white sugar. A splash of low fat milk. By eleven, I made her Jack and Coke. Three ice cubes. She guzzled so many liquids her liver could swim laps in her abdomen. These San Francisco doctors underestimated my mom, a tough one who could always get back in the saddle.

"Let's get out of here. I'm starving," she said.

"Me too." My step-dad left us to go find food alone. Mom casually pulled on some pants and a brown jacket with two shell buttons. Her legs were more spindly and puckered than I remembered. And she was jaundiced. We walked out an emergency exit down some stairs, like a team.

On Fillmore Street, the sun was bright and the wind was chilly. We strolled into a bookstore. My mom, a speed-reader who typed sixty words per minute, grabbed *The Easter Parade*. We sat on a bench inside a bagel shop with a big window and watched shoppers stroll up and down Fillmore as the fog wrapped around the tops of Victorians like foam. We sipped tomato soup from paper bowls. Our elbows touched.

"It's not as good as mine," she said.

"No, of course not."

"Too salty. And it needs some of my delicious basil." Her greenhouse exploded with orange and red heirlooms year round. I loved to get tangled in their wiry vines, dust off the ripe ones on my T-shirt, and pop them in my mouth. I would fill my arms and shirt with the rest to slice and drizzle with her signature vinaigrette. She grew zucchini big as baseball bats and green apples cluttered her lawn. The ones she didn't bake in crisps and cobblers were fed to her horses. Neighbors came with empty arms and left with Ziploc bags full of Mom's fruit.

I told her about the migration habits of cicadas, how they molted their old skin, became new again. She looked at me, puzzled.

"I got fired from the law firm," I said.

"It's okay, honey. You'll get another job."

"I'm stripping again," I said, even though it wasn't exactly true yet. I knew it soon would be. She stroked my back, like I was a cat.

WE WALKED THROUGH THE thick fog back to the hospital, where she got undressed and climbed back into bed. A nurse folded her arms in front on her chest.

"This isn't a hotel," she said sternly. Mom chuckled. "I'm fine. Go back home." I hugged her close, shuffled out the exit and stepped into the moist San Francisco night.

ON THE DRIVE BACK to L.A., tension pressed down on my ribcage. *She's fine.*

I went jogging like the runners I'd envied every morning on my commute. I had to breathe when I jogged. I couldn't cry and run at the same time. I refused music and shunned podcasts. Silence allowed me to count: three minutes of warm up at a pace of 3.9. I was aware of every muscle in my back. My knee clicked. *Give up later.* Five minutes in, I forced my legs to speed up to a pace of 5.7. I trotted. Eighteen minutes in, drop your shoulders, relax your neck. Forty minutes later, weightless and calm; I could run for hours. Worry poured out of me like radio waves. Pools of sunlight glittered on the surface of the reservoir. Three minutes of cool down.

When the phone rang, I raced to get it.

"It's not my liver," Mom said.

"Oh?" I laughed.

"I have a cancer so rare, it's like getting struck by lightning," she said. "It's pretty early stage. An-eee-ways, they're doing Whipple surgery."

"Should I come?"

"In a couple weeks, when I'm home." She was logical, reasonable, and organized. She didn't want to inconvenience me.

I asked, "What kind of cancer?" But she'd already hung up.

Whipple sounded like pie topping, but, according to Ask.com, it was a surgery performed for patients with bile duct cancer. It involved cutting open Mom's stomach, removing her intestines, spreading them out on the table like a ribbon, scraping the cancer off and stuffing them back inside. After Whipple surgery, eating solid food would be a novelty. Chances of heart or liver failure were high. *She'll be fine*, I thought, defiantly, but I held my belly tightly as the tension weighed down on my body.

Her chemo and radiation treatments started. Her phone messages stopped. She mailed me recipes she'd found in magazines with handwritten notes in her perfect, paralegal script: "Great and Easy!" I cooked only her yellow dishes. I perfected lemon bars with shortbread crust and labored over whipped egg whites for banana soufflé. I peeled off her Post-it notes and tacked them onto my kitchen cupboards for inspiration while I sifted flour and squeezed juice from lemons. My floor was sticky with powdered sugar. I crammed my kitchen counters with trays of her dessert then watched it all spoil.

# 32

*A*FTER FIVE ABDOMINAL SURGERIES, chemo, and radiation, she marched back into the elections department like a superhero. "They let me do whatever I want now," she said. My sturdy mom was well again. Her co-workers who used to bug her, she told me, could kiss her horse-loving ass. There'd be birthdays to celebrate and trips to Costa Rica. There'd be a future. Christmas trees. Now, there was hope and there was time. Remission was a promise of walks on the beach and jaunts to the farmer's market, photographing sunsets from her beautiful redwood deck.

"Yeah. My cancer markers are nil," she said, buzzing on hope. The two of us sighed on the phone. *Remission. See? We dared believe.*

I'd been up to Humboldt and back several times during her treatments. Even with health insurance, Mom's hospital bills drained her bank accounts. She considered selling her property—the property that was supposed to be my inheritance.

During that time, I also auditioned for a reality television show.

"If I win, I'll give you half the prize money," I promised her. I wasn't the girl who won things, but I imagined the look on her face if I did. So I about peed myself when I was chosen to be a contestant to appear on the show for the twenty-five thousand dollar cash prize. "I'm going to be on the show!" I told Mom.

"See?" She said. "You can do anything."

I waited in a chair backstage. Eight judges sat on a panel deciding whom to give the prize to, based on questions they asked us. They weren't allowed to ask contestants about their financial situation, but they could ask us anything else and reject us on a whim. The panelists were chosen from all over the U.S. The contestants were considered "extreme" in terms of their lifestyle. There was a puppeteer with HIV, a pregnant Mormon woman on her ninth child, a preacher from Michigan, and a Madame from Vegas who carried a binder with pictures of her stable of hookers.

The producer, a plucky brunette named Jen who cracked jokes all day long, led me by the elbow to the judges for the third time that day. It was between me and one other guy, a kid from Laguna who lived with his fisherman Dad.

"You're about to win a lot of money," Heather whispered to me. Mom was going to be so thrilled. I savored just the thought of that conversation: "Mom, I have fantastic news."

"What?" She'd say.

"Oh nothing. You can keep your property."

Onstage, the hot lights were brutal. "Do you think prostitution should be legal?" A short gay guy with short spiky hair asked me.

"Of course. It's a victimless crime," I said, cupping my right hand over my eyes. The glare was blinding.

"Where did you get your clothes? They look like they're straight off the rack from Melrose." What did he care if I bought my clothes from Melrose? I told the truth.

"A girl gave them to me for organizing her closet." Organizing closets was one of my side gigs. I'd salvaged cool stuff lately from garbage bags meant for Goodwill, a fringe benefit when a client had parted with her old clothes. I rifled through the bags and took what I wanted.

"So, people just hand you stuff? That shirt looks brand new." The lights were so bright I thought my skin would boil. I could only make out the short guy's spiky blonde hair. *What was his fucking problem?* I wanted to hose him down. The surfer kid was completely relaxed while I was being grilled.

I said, "People don't hand me stuff. I work for stuff." A bead of sweat dripped from my temple. I took off my jacket and held it to keep from melting.

"Why did you hide those tattoos from us?" he asked.

"You've seen them. They're all over my portfolio." I hit back. Mom had helped me by compiling pictures for a profile for the show. He shrugged as if to suggest, "See? She's a big fat liar." Guilt gushed through me. Even when accused of something I didn't do, I buzzed with adrenaline and shame. The relaxed kid answered a tame question about wearing real fur. He refused to do it. The judges gave the $25K to the kid who lived with his parents and drove a surfer van because he didn't wear real fur. My face burned. I was crushed, and Mom's property was sold.

I thought about how different my life looked only a couple of months before when Rico, my friend Gina's regular client, took me to lunch at Casa Vega. Like the strip clubs, Casa Vega was a dark, private place to wheel and deal. The bar was packed with men who were well into their second or third scotch.

I didn't know why Rico wanted to meet me there. I'd only met him once before. Rico found Gina in the adult gigs section of Craigslist after she posted topless photos of herself in a meth-inspired attempt to find a sugar daddy. She needed help. She had a couple of DUIs and was seeking quick cash. Rico took Gina on a sixty thousand dollar shopping trip to Versace and flew her to St. Barths and Brazil, but there was a price she had to pay. There always is.

Rico waved at me from the bar and slipped the host a hundred dollar bill. The host led us to Rico's special table in the back. I sunk deep in the plush red seats, which were very much like the lap dancing couches in strip clubs I'd known. After a long silence, I said, "My mom thinks I should go back to grad school."

"You should," he responded. "Get that Masters for your mom. I'll pay for it." He sipped Diet Coke from a skinny red cocktail straw. He ate cheese quesadillas and dunked warm tortilla chips into salsa. He wasn't a dainty eater.

"You have my word," he said. He handed me a thousand dollars in cash under the table. Pecked me on the cheek.

"Just fax me the paperwork," he said. I faxed it seventeen times and called him ten. I never heard from Rico again.

# 33

"MEET ME NEAR THE big fish tank near the entrance," Spaceship Steve texted. Kara needed a night off, and I needed some fast cash so she set up an appointment for me with one of her regulars, a professional gambler who was on a winning streak at Commerce Casino. She said his energy was tapped into another realm—so much so that when she jerked him off, she felt transported to a Sheryl Crow concert, so he became Spaceship Steve. I had nothing against Sheryl Crow, so I agreed.

Besides, Mom had called.

"I didn't sleep at all last night, but I don't want to go to the hospital again," she said.

"You're okay, mom. You just had a bad night." She was just being dramatic.

There was the casino, blinking its gaudy eyes, right off the freeway.

"You need to come say goodbye," she said. I heard her blow her nose.

"Mom, you'll feel fine later. Take a nap."

"When can you get here?" she asked. I pulled into the dark parking garage.

"Soon, Mom." She was sick again. The cancer was back.

Stupid. I clocked my outfit. I forgot that Kara had instructed me to dress down. She said that when hooking, you should dress like a celebrity going to the gym on her day off: ripped jeans and a hoodie. Converse tennis shoes. A loose ponytail. I looked like a hooker meeting a trick in a sexy black slip dress that showed my lace, rhinestone bra and fishnets. Seriously stupid, I thought, walking towards the sliding glass doors. Icy wind from the air conditioner hit my bare arms. I wandered around aimlessly. The casino was packed with Asian men. I wondered what card game they were playing. Just when I was about to pivot back out the door, I spotted the huge aquarium full of striped fish, swimming lazily.

A big white guy with a red baseball cap tapped away on his blackberry. He looked up. "Steve?" I asked quietly. He nodded and hugged me like an old friend.

"Let's walk this way," he said and led me to an elevator. We got off on the fourth floor and walked down a burgundy hallway to his tiny room, with two small twin beds. "How'd you do tonight?"

"Pretty good," he said.

"Do you stay here a lot?" I asked, removing my slip quickly.

"When I come to town," he said. "Two hundred, right?" He handed me the bills. He was a doughy, freckled man with red hair. I walked over to him and pressed my boobs and belly against him. "Oh, I want an actual massage, too, if that's okay."

"Of course," I said. Shit. Spaceship Steve is going to take the whole hour, I thought.

"Do you always win?" I asked him.

"Sometimes," he said. I pulled off the cheap Aztec comforter and motioned for him to lie down on the sheets.

I took out my fourteen-dollar almond oil and poured a generous amount on his pimply back. Steve was already naked and on his stomach. My hands moved down to his chubby calves and slowly up his inner thighs. He had a smattering of pimples across his upper back. I needed him to hurry.

Mom's fevers were back. *Cancer markers, T-cell counts, DNR, DNI, chemo, radiation, infection, five abdominal surgeries, PEG-tube, remission, metastasis, septicemia, organ failure, hospice care, and morphine drip. It all starts again.*

I had to get to Mom and take her to her chemo then hold the bucket so she could puke. Get her a warm washcloth for her face when she cried. Give my step-dad Chris a break. Bile Duct Cancer loves Gallbladder Cancer loves Pancreatic Cancer. Mom loved horses. They bucked her off. She got back up.

"How's that feel?" I asked with my fingers lingering on his wet balls, slick from the oil. He turned over, cock like a kickstand. I grabbed it. He removed my hand.

"Slow down." I needed him to hurry. I needed Mom to be okay.

"I'll go slow," I said. "Promise."

My happiest moments with Mom were spent in a moldy old library when I was eight or nine. "You ready to go?" she hollered from the kitchen and I ran upstairs with my orange corduroy book bag. At the library, we took our time looking at books and flipping through the dusty pages. I grabbed all the Judy Blume and Beverly Cleary books I could carry and lugged them all up to the counter, plopped them down. "Are you really going to read all those?" she asked with a disbelieving look. Her arms were crossed in front of her chest.

"Mmmhm," I said.

"You have to carry them all yourself." Her gray eyes twinkled. She was playing mad. I piled the ones that didn't fit in my bag into my arms like logs, carried them to her seventy-four forest-green Volvo, and tossed them onto the backseat. I didn't know then what words and stories would mean to me. I had no idea they would grow long alien arms and wrap around me and show me the sky and the galaxy and beyond. Books would change my stripes and make me cry and sink into my skull. Books excited me. They were a way out of my crummy small town, and they were something I shared with Mom. We took our time in the library.

My hand was on Steve's cock, jerking him off. "Slower," he said. He placed my hands on his ass. I let my fingers linger there and massaged his balls again, annoyed. The room was stuffy and dark and had a view of long tall buildings; a room where secrets happened.

After the first round of chemo, Mom tried eating a steak and had to return to the hospital. Her body couldn't break down meat anymore. She had a fever, another infection. She had to use the feeding tube again. I had to get back to her. I needed this Sheryl Crow concert to end.

I poured more oil on Steve's cock and tightened my grip. "Are you ready to go?" I asked him and made him come hard, exploding all over his pudgy stomach. I put on my slinky black lace dress and walked out of the Casino into the hot, dry air. I couldn't remember where I'd parked my car. I wandered in the garage for fifteen minutes, dazed. Just like Mom had in Vegas, years before.

On the drive back to my apartment, I pretended what happened didn't really happen at all. I shoved some clothes into a suitcase and stared at it.

Before she got sick again, Mom had said, "Go get that degree, honey." She insisted I go to grad school, which felt like an unlikely luxury, one that I didn't deserve. The other students had families and jobs and were already authors and teachers. I felt like I was from another planet–thirty-seven years old and no great achievements or jobs skills. To pick up books again and write full time seemed extravagant. Maybe if I got my Master's, Mom would live longer. She'd be able to drink a toast with her neighbor, Charlene. She'd say, "My daughter got her Master's," and in my small way, I would give her something to be proud of. Even though I knew an MFA degree wouldn't guarantee a career or make me more employable, it would make me an unusually articulate sex worker. And that was something.

# 34

"*J* FEEL LIKE HELL. WHEN are you coming home?" Mom's voice sounded as if her cheeks were stuffed with Kleenex, a muffled tune of giving up. I needed to talk to her in person about not giving up, but I was on the 210 Freeway, speeding towards Pleasures, the only topless bar in Pasadena. "Soon, Mom."

I didn't have enough money to go see her. Shit, I didn't have enough money to feed myself. Any work I'd had, all my mini-gigs, had dried up. People left town, people hired someone else, someone cheaper. Bunny wasn't answering her phone, Fred was out of town. It felt like work was allergic to me. That, or I'd somehow screwed my karma. I had an eighth a tank of gas and eighteen dollars, ten of which I blew on cat food.

"Hang on, Mom." I spotted Pleasures across the street from a used car dealership, tossed my phone in my lap and pulled in. It was time to strip again, but I was geriatric in stripper years. I'd heard Pleasures was the kind of place that wouldn't have a problem with that.

Gas prices were astronomical, creeping over four-thirty a gallon, and it's a twelve-hour haul to Humboldt from Los Angeles, so I decided to fly instead. It's faster. *Sink or swim*, knowing that the best swimmers always drown. It's the panic and fatigue of suffocation, not mechanical skills, that kill. The trick is to calm down and breathe, conserve energy.

"I'll see you soon, Mom," I said and hung up. I lugged my pink Victoria's Secret bag full of my remaining costumes through a door that was propped open with a brick. There's something awful about entering a strip club with the bright Los Angeles sun still blazing overhead. It's like wearing a down ski jacket in hundred-degree weather or sitting in a hot tub wrapped in fur.

The heat reminded me of Vegas, and Vegas reminded me of cancer. Vegas reminded me of Mom's cancer. I marched into Pleasures and said, "I'm here to audition," to a short guy who was frying meat. Later, he would try to sell me a copy of his book, *Beyond the Pole*. He flipped the burger and lifted a ceramic white plate off the top of a stack, set it on the metal surface, and sliced a pale, mealy tomato wedge, poured salt on it, and popped it into his mouth. His meat sizzled. I wiped sweat from my upper lip. Tiny clouds of grease hit his forearm.

"Get dressed then bring me your ID," he said, glancing up at me.

Pleasures was larger than it looked on their website. There was a stage in the middle of the room with a rusty, slim pole, and a pool table with a long bar. The only way to the dressing room was through the kitchen. I held my pink bag to my chest in order to fit through. It stuck to my sweaty arms and made a ripping sound when I pulled it free and dropped in on the floor of the dinky dressing room. I peeled off my jeans and checked out my thirty-seven-year-old flab in the cracked, spotted mirror. It had been four years since I'd stripped. Four years and my edges had blurred—my hipbones covered with thick cellulite. The shock of seeing my flaws under fluorescent lights filled me with embarrassment. I squeezed into one remaining pair of shiny booty shorts as I'd done a thousand times before, though never after such a long hiatus. I'd been busy bulging out while Mom had been shrinking. My thick softness betrayed how I felt: sharp, tight, and breathless. I faced the mirror next to girls young enough to be my daughters.

I angrily grabbed Lucite shoes from my bag in their smelly, scuffed, six-inch glory, which helped with the fat problem. Taller is the optical illusion for thinner. Next came a faded, sparkling, borrowed pink bikini that smelled like stale bubble gum.

I was not only heavier than the other two dancers, with their legs like blades of snake grass and slim, pointy ankles; I was older, much older. They were maybe twenty-five, but their fake reading glasses, white knee socks, and plaid miniskirts screamed teen porn star. They had names that dripped nasty barely-legal sex like Hennessy and Bijou. One had braces. She bared her teeth and picked something from them, showing flesh toned rubber bands stretching the length of her wet, open mouth. Another girl would look icky doing such a thing, but she looked luscious. I wanted to put my whole hand in her mouth, just to prop it open. I smeared gloppy pink lipstick over my lips and pressed powder over my face to conceal the dark circles under my eyes. I pressed foundation into the tiny lines along my temples.

I found the short guy in an office next to a silver metal file cabinet confiscated from a garage sale in the seventies. I handed him my California license and he made a copy. "If you get onstage now, you can work tonight." He handed back my ID, looked at his watch, and walked towards the bar. I was relieved to be one of the only girls working the 4:00 P.M. shift on a Monday.

I walked right up to the DJ and gave him a huge smile. "I'm Angelique," I said and wrote it on his list, which is the equivalent of punching a time clock at a nine to five.

He nodded. "Angelique it is," he said and took a swig of his sweaty Budweiser.

The kitchen inside Pleasures smelled like rat shit and frozen hamburger. I walked around the empty room in the darkness, looking for a lap to fall into. It was like I'd never stopped. Three hundred bucks and I could pack tonight. Leave in the morning. Catch a flight through San Francisco. I introduced myself to a bald guy who called himself Old Joe. He drank neat whiskey and told me he had nothing in his head but marbles. Old Joe introduced me to the guy in the wheelchair.

"This is Tripod."

"Why Tripod?"

"Because he has two long arms and a huge hard-on," Old Joe said. Tripod had polio. I liked him right away because he was cocky and unfazed, determined to enjoy himself. His greasy beer smell came from a bender that had started in Vegas, and that bender was petering out during my first shift at Pleasures.

"Tripod, what's the situation here?" I asked. "How about a dance?"

"Do whatever you want with me," he grinned lopsided. I was determined to make a hundred bucks off Tripod.

"Step into my office," I said and led him to the lap dancing area, a room with gum-stained black couches and oil-spotted red carpet. Dancers writhing in front of their customers gave me looks when Tripod rolled his wheelchair in next to them. He did another shot while I waited for the next song to start. I rubbed my chest in his face and imagined being in Humboldt with my mom in the redwoods. I remembered summers spent with just her and I and our books, sunning ourselves in Willow Creek, leaving only when the shadows grew long and dark. I had to be next to her again. I needed Tripod to hurry.

After a few songs with Tripod, I went to the bathroom to count my cash. I sat on the toilet to escape the loud music and decided how much longer I needed to remain at Pleasures. In the stall next to me a girl in plastic heels scuffed the floor, then snorted. "Shit," she said.

The girls were really fucked-up at Pleasures. Taped on the bathroom stall door was a Xerox copy of some girl's driver's license with a scribbled note that said she died in a drunk driving accident and there would be a memorial. She was twenty-three. I looked closely at her dark eyes and petite nose while I counted bills, but her features were so blurry, she could have been any of us. None of the girls mentioned the dead girl, and they still got hammered before driving away from Pleasures.

One hundred twenty bucks. I needed more. I approached a guy in a Bob Dylan T-shirt whose name was McKenzie. He swerved standing up and finally settled into the smoking area, where I followed him. "Let's get out of here," he said. "I have a place." I thought of my mom's soft voice saying, "I'm barely here." My skin rattled to the beat of the bass. I was anxious to get enough dough to bail and if that meant doing more, then to hell with it.

"Let's discuss it in a dance." I pulled McKenzie towards the red vinyl couch and he collapsed. He handed me a crumpled twenty.

I spread his knees apart and wriggled between them.

"Tell me about your place," I said.

"I have keys to a preschool where I'm doing construction," he said. He slurred his words.

"Where's this school?" I danced around him, and brushed my hair in his face.

"Just meet me at the ATM across the street," he said. "I'll give you three hundred."

I looked around, panicked someone had heard us. "It's in Glendale, a couple miles from here," he said. I looked at my watch. It was nearly midnight.

"One more dance," I said. I needed to think about what I was about to do.

"No. I don't want another dance." He handed me sixty bucks. "Meet me across the street." I took the cash.

"Give me fifteen minutes," I said. I checked out and paid my stage fee. The impulses weren't familiar anymore, a new desperation had settled into my bones. In my car, I drove slowly across the street into a shopping plaza, where there was indeed a Bank of America ATM, and looked around nervously.

McKenzie was smoking a cigarette. He seemed more sober suddenly. He took out the cash. I was right next to him with my hand out. I reached for it. He snapped it away. "After." Then he said, "Ride with me."

"No way." I daydreamed about lunging into oncoming traffic, but not before seeing my mom.

"Follow me." He walked to his white flatbed construction truck. I waited in my car until I saw him pass and followed him to Glendale for about eight minutes. We exited onto a quiet suburban street with parked hybrids and jacaranda blossoms splattered on the ground. I parked and watched him maneuver slowly into a tight parking space in front of me.

A man got out of the white truck and glared at me. He walked to a porch and stood with his fists clenched at his sides, then disappeared into the house and slammed his front door. Only, this man wasn't McKenzie. I drove away with my one eighty from Pleasures and laughed until my gut hurt.

The next day, I was applying eyeliner in the dressing room at Pleasures, when my phone rang.

"What now?" I asked Mom.

"I'm in the hospital. It came back," she said. Her voice was raspy.

"What do we do now?" I said. Something dark raged in me. *Fuck everyone who's not my mom.*

"Take me home."

# 35

*I*N MY SMALL COASTAL California hometown, a storm had caused an electrical outage. I drove through thick-as-cotton Arcata fog, careful at the wheel. Visibility was so bad that I couldn't see the shabby farmhouses and lazy cows telling me I was home, but I stared hard until I felt it. Rain spat bullets on my windows, and seagulls flew through the downpour. I thought maybe the white birds meant good news, like they do in Hallmark cards. They meant she would get well. When I pulled up to the hospital, it was nearly dark, running on a lame generator. The hospital looked shabby and unkempt, and this pissed me off to no end. Her room smelled like Pleasures: bleach and air freshener and there was a Christmas tree with a wimpy strand of gold garland and small red bulbs that hung from its branches. That tree infuriated me. *What do they know?* She brightened when she saw me, held up her wrist to wave me over.

"I like your new watch," I said.

"You can't have it."

"Why not?"

"Because it's mine." She giggled. Morphine made everything silly and fuzzy.

I sat close to her and told her about my lemon bars. "Not as good as yours," I said. I touched her hand. She winced.

"It hurts to move," she said. I walked over to the Christmas tree, removed the bald garland, and rearranged the stupid bulbs so they were all towards the front.

"That's better," I said. She wrinkled her nose at me. My step-dad hovered in the background.

She moaned when she sat up. Every time she did, my chest clenched. She couldn't stand without me holding her. On the slow walk to the car, she held her elbow in the air. "Wait. No diapers. If I piss myself, that's it. Promise me."

At home, under a thick, pink blanket, in a room that was once used as her office, she puked her guts out all day long. Her neon orange vomit filled the bucket I held for her. When I was not rinsing that bucket, I sat in her office chair and typed on her computer. "I like that sound," she said.

Chris rummaged in the kitchen for a lighter and appeared in the doorway. "She's on a lot of morphine," he said. I figured this meant the job of sorting through the boxes of family photos would be mine. It's a thing we'd discussed on the phone several times, a thing we'd put off again and again. She wanted to go through the albums one last time, tell me the secrets they held. There'd be photos of hillbillies with long fingers, tanned skin and big noses. Wide foreheads like mine. I was ready to listen.

Chris opened a window, lit a Marlboro, and stared outside towards the sand, ocean, and pasture. He leaned into the fresh cold air with bewildered, gray eyes, and blew smoke. Beside Mom on the table was a glass of ice water with a bendy straw and a purple candle, flickering. It smelled like baby powder. She rocked forward slightly as though she were engulfed in thick syrup; she was unrecognizable.

"Can't we take her off that shit?" I sat on a table directly across from her, but she looked past me. Albums were in a pile on the floor along with bags of pictures in white envelopes, all labeled and dated meticulously. I held up a picture of Mom in a garden picking strawberries. She was about sixteen years old, an honor student with reading glasses decorated with rhinestones. She wore her light brown hair short and her even white teeth held the promise of fresh breath. She could've been the face of Dentyne gum. She stood near a fence, holding a fat red strawberry. "Look, Mom," I said. She stared at it for a long time but didn't recognize the girl in the photo.

Mom was happy in the dirt. She loved gardening. My childhood was spent picking blueberries, peas, tomatoes, zucchini, and huckleberries from the backyard. Jars of blackberry jam with shiny gold lids; rhubarb and honey were poured over vanilla ice cream. Summers were spent in the bushes, picking peas and blackberries. I plucked cherry tomatoes from vines. I found a picture of me wiping tomato seeds on my jeans. I remembered how I bit into the fruit and how seeds squirted my T-shirts.

"That's not my mom," I said, staring into her unfocused eyes, then put my hand on hers.

"The pain gets worse and worse," Chris said.

"Take her off of it. We need to talk."

A long silence, then "alright." He blew more smoke and stood against the wall by the window. We didn't give her any more morphine for the rest of that day or night. I barely slept through her moaning.

The room that used to be her office still looked the same—square and dinky with pale, peach walls like the lipsticks Mom and I used to order from Avon catalogs in the early eighties. The pink lipsticks I wanted had names like Melon Crunch and Sugar Breeze. On one wall, was a picture of Mom dressed in a brown pantsuit with a silky striped scarf. When I was about nine, I stood in her walk-in closet and watched her dress for work. I studied her orderly and mysterious system, careful to stay out of her way. Her taupe polyester vest exactly matched her short, snug, secretary skirt. I was crazy about her legs. My legs were chunky, muscular, tap-dancing stumps compared to her slim horseback-riding calves. Mom's slender thighs stretched and floated as she twirled in the full-length mirror. We both admired her legs shimmering and stretching in Hanes control top panty hose. She layered her pink and brown lipsticks to make just the right shade of bronze. I wanted Mom's lips, so I smeared her pink stain all over my mouth, which turned my lips orange. She giggled. "That's it." She brushed pink powder on my cheeks and sent me off to school like that. I watched her curl her thick hair into meticulous brown waves. Those mornings, I learned how to be a girl.

On another corkboard were postcards from Spain. Mom took a trip with her friends and brought me back two small ceramic bowls with blue flowers painted on them. Next to the Spain pictures, snapshots of her cats: Willow and Sam dozing in her rhubarb plants. In the background were the two elegant, brown horses; one of them was blind.

The tan office carpet had new groove marks where the feeding tube rolled and beeped. The beep was louder than an alarm clock, a jarring, horrible sound. The little robot feeding tube pumped neon pink-orange fluid into my mom's stomach through a red, angry hole. Under pink-coral blankets, her eyelashes fluttered and her hands clasped shut in front of her chest. She wore her wedding ring. She wore her watch. She wore fuzzy pink-striped socks. She wanted to read the paper. I handed it to her.

On her outdated computer, I had translated a Finnish poem about springtime and flute music and being in love. It was neither springtime nor was I in love; it was an assignment for school. The instructor posted recordings of the poems being read in Finnish; certain hints of words meant *to wake up thick with dreams.*

Awake, she said, "Can I have a glass of water?" I held a glass of ice water with a straw that was long enough to reach her mouth without her having to move her head much. I stretched it out and made sure it wouldn't dribble water down her chin. That would've irked her. She hated messes. It dribbled, and I dabbed her chin with a paper towel.

Her face had more spider veins than I remembered. Her hair had grown back gray and thin. Her shapely legs had shriveled to toothpicks. I held the blue glass to her mouth, and she sipped the milk. "I'm too hot," she said.

She pushed the melon colored comforter aside and threw up white curdled milk on the blankets. I grabbed more paper towels. Warmed a washcloth in the sink. Held it to her forehead. Her hair was damp from sweat. The fever was back. On the desk was a pile of bills and files. She used to keep papers in meticulous paralegal-style order, but now everything was in disarray. The afternoon sun faded to fog. I opened the window.

She was clammy. Her eyes now focused and clear.

"I'm dying," she said.

"I know." I wanted to cry, but I just sat there stiff as a redwood.

The next afternoon, when she was asleep, I crept into the kitchen, opened the refrigerator, and grabbed a tub of fat-free Cool Whip, using my fingers as a scoop until my mouth overflowed with the low calorie white foam. I chased it with half a package of semisweet chocolate chips. Then I went for the pumpkin pie that was still in the package. I hated pumpkin pie. I ate three pieces in four minutes. *You're disgusting.*

I walked back into the office where Mom dozed and slid the window open a crack to allow the chilly wet air to sweep through the room, until she protested the cold. I fussed over the daffodils her neighbor, Charlene, brought over, and I casually changed her sheets, hoping she didn't notice she'd peed the bed. I held a cool washcloth to her forehead. "Am I going to the bathroom?" she asked, but it came out like an accusation. She asked again. "Am I?"

I wanted to lie, but her sad, gray marble eyes knew mine too well. I washed her hair in the kitchen sink with vanilla-scented shampoo. The warm water was nearly hot, but she shivered anyway. Outside, her horses snorted and dug their hooves into the mud.

I wrapped a dry towel around her head like a turban and I led her by her bony hands back to the bed.

"I wish I could be your best friend for longer," she said.

"Me too."

"You promised," she said, reminding me of our agreement, as if I had forgotten. I felt inept. I didn't know finality except what I'd seen on television: villains folded in half from a neat, single gunshot, dancing in slow motion, then collapsing softly in a small puddle of stage blood. This wasn't that. "I don't want to die," she said.

"Maybe you won't die, Mom. Maybe you'll get better." I gave her my best smile and forced myself to look into her eyes, so deep with loneliness. I kept my sorrow hidden, stored away for a more convenient time when I could feel things. I dried her hair. She sat up.

"Do it, but don't tell me when you have done it. I want to go to sleep and never wake up."

"Does Chris know?"

"We talked."

"I want to be cremated," she said. "Write this down." I took dictation: "Royal blue glass vases, purple and blue napkins. Irises, lilies, lemon bars, tea. Chocolate chip bars. I want it overlooking the Humboldt Bay, in the afternoon. Let me write the guest list," she said, stroking the corner of my yellow legal pad. I handed her a pencil and, in her graceful, paralegal script, she wrote the names of friends and songs to play. At the bottom of the page, she wrote, "Her strength was her heart." She was a speechwriter and straight A achiever. She kept a tight lid on her chaos. My childhood was neatly stacked and color coordinated. Mom taught me the simple algebra of love and order, but there was no order here.

I walked in circles and stared into space for hours. Chris found me in the kitchen holding the vials of morphine.

"Are you sure?" he asked. He smoked a Marlboro and squinted into space through exhausted, craggy eyes. He was flipping through a travel book for Costa Rica.

"We planned to take this trip as soon as she was strong enough," he said. He looked like he hadn't slept for a year.

"Do you have enough morphine in the house?"

"We can't undo it once it's done," he said. "Enough there to kill ten horses."

"What if we get caught?"

"I spoke to her doctor. No autopsy. I can't keep doing this. We talked about it. I'll lose everything." Fire burned the backs of my calves. I heard her voice from the other room. I could hear her pain getting worse. Feel it eclipsing the whole house. I was silent, but her moaning was getting louder. She was too proud to be kept alive in a puddle of orange piss. _What a fucking rip-off._ "This goes into the feeding tube. Directly into her bloodstream," he said, between drags. "Press this," the syringe was fat and clear.

"I don't want to hate her," he said.

_You don't already?_ He'd taken weeks off work to make the trips to San Francisco for surgeries and treatments. Weeks in and out of hospitals to sit by her side.

We walked into the bedroom where Mom was sleeping. I emptied one syringe into the feeding tube and another one into the same spot and he put his hand over mine. I didn't look at him. My other hand was holding her hand, which was folded across her stomach. She didn't wince from my touch now.

The room shrunk with the heat of our bodies waiting for death. A few moments passed but nothing happened. Chris pushed another vial into the tube. One after the other, and another, until we had emptied several. We watched her eyelids, listened to her breathe, but her chest kept swelling with breath. I played soft music so she could drift into a familiar tune and get sucked under. It continued for hours.

At three in the morning, my step-dad said, "If she doesn't stop breathing, we'll put a pillow over her face."

"I can't."

"But she'll die in our arms."

I walked out of the room, collapsed on the brown couch that still held the indentations of her body.

The clock said 4:12 A.M. when I heard my step-dad say, "She's not breathing anymore." He wrung his hands and paced in front of the fireplace, then walked downstairs to the bedroom they had shared for eighteen years. I needed Mom's legs. In the cold room, I saw that he had removed her wedding band. I played with her toes. She still wore her fuzzy, pink, striped socks. I placed my hand on top of her stiff thighs and kissed them.

She was white as Arcata fog.

I THOUGHT I'D SCREAM and there'd be blood everywhere. I thought cymbals would crash. Lightning would strike. I'd throw a bottle at a window and make it rain glass shards. I'd be on the ground, writhing, run to the sea naked and jump into the freezing sea. But none of that happened. Not by a long shot.

Death is more like the ocean, tired and heavy and cold.

I borrowed Chris' truck—I needed to get out, to drive, to be alone; I didn't know what I needed, I didn't know shit, but I wanted my mom.

I flipped an illegal U-turn. That's when I got pulled over. After the cop left, I sat on a wet stone and waited for the ocean to show me what me-without-Mom looked like. *Would it make me walk with a limp? Would I cry? Would it be like walking with no arms?* I waved my arms around. The new alone was a big silence that floated around me like mist, but the nuts and bolts of losing you took years to sink in.

# Part 5

*"Come get me out of here."*

# 36

ACK IN MY L.A. apartment I was digging through Mom's photo albums, looking for a joyful memory of her to replace the image I had in my mind of her barfing up milk and wasting away on urine-soaked sheets.

One of her albums was from the seventies. It was half full and called "Baby's Milestones: Birth to Seven Years." The empty half of it was full of illustrations of squiggly babies where pictures were supposed to go and blank lines for describing them. She had taped, cut, and pasted the photos with a fastidiousness that bordered on obsession. She even wound a creepy lock of my dishwater-blonde hair on a page titled "first haircut." She added other notes about my budding personality in her poised, secretarial handwriting, like "Antonia is very sneaky."

Evidently, I was born sneaky. It's right there, on my six months page. *What was I trying to sneak at six months old? My stuffed Miss Piggy? What did I want so badly that I had to attempt to fool my mom in order to get it?* On other pages, in cursive blue ink, she recorded my weight, height, and the shots that the doctors gave me every three months. She ripped and glued a ratty beige square from my baby blanket. She listed the ice cream I favored (chocolate) and my first word (Dada). She commented that I didn't cry much, even when she most expected me to, like at the doctor's, or on trips. By six months old I was a trooper, prepared for an emotional showdown.

Nine long months passed before I said "Mama," according to her notes. On that page, Mom noted that I "cried very loudly when slapped."

After one year, she stopped recording. Blank pages followed, as if I'd disappeared. But really, she probably just returned to work full time. She was a paralegal and in at least three women's organizations. She had shit to do.

MOM KEPT MY WRINKLED report cards from Kindergarten, first, and second grades from the private Catholic school I attended, shoved in between the pages of the photo album. My gross baby hair spilled out. Seeing the report cards again revealed another theme—I had low self-regard and shaky confidence. "Needs encouragement," one nun wrote. "Needs to gain self-confidence." Math made me cry, but much of my bewilderment was religion. The bulk of my early education was singing songs about the blood of Christ. Clapping along with repeat phrases about lambs and blood and traitors. I enjoyed Mass with the blue and purple stained glass windows and the shiny deep brown pews. It was a giant place of sunlight and peacefulness. Sometimes, it was a little scary with the man in white holding that huge cup in the air and waving it in circles. Thing was, we weren't even Catholic. We belonged to a Baptist Church that was brown, chilly, and full of old people. We dropped in for tune-ups during the popular holidays. I attended bible school where I made wobbly structures out of yarn and Popsicle sticks with the other kids, and kissed my first boy, an older freckled ginger named Roger.

In the photo albums were pictures of a Hawaiian vacation we took when I was about twelve. The trip wasn't just a vacation: my svelte hunk of a big brother lived there at the time, working as a cook. He'd been happy while in Hawaii and was thrilled to see us all: aunts, uncles, and my pretty, valedictorian, cheerleading cousins. A clan. Years later, he'd be hooked on drugs and spend most of his adult life in prison or homeless in a van with his infant daughter. One night in Hawaii, when the adults were inside the rented house drinking, I plotted sneaking out. My plan was to meet the local blonde surfer guy I'd met on the beach and make out with him.

I crept out alone and was surprised to find him, sitting on a rock under the stars in bare feet, like he'd said he would be. I didn't know how old he was. He'd taught my cousin how to surf the day before. I kissed him for a long time but didn't know what came next. I got scared and ran back inside the house where my family was sleeping.

Here is the photograph. Mom is beautiful and tan and lounges on a chair, reading with a floppy, blue sun hat on her head and big, dark sunglasses. Her shapely, toned legs are strong. I want to be as smart and pretty as she is. I'm struck by the geography of her face: her strong jaw, her straight teeth and regal nose. We look alike: our long arms and slim hands. We tan the same deep brown, our pale Irish skin nuanced by Algonquin Indian gold tones. I don't have her beautiful legs. I have her eyes.

In the Hawaii pictures, I look exactly like my mom in the face, with one difference: I smiled to conceal my discomfort. She smiled when things were going well.

# 37

ACK AT PLEASURES, I grabbed the pole, hoisted myself upside down, and stared into my blue gray eyes in the mirror. They looked like my Mom's, except mine were wild with rage. I buzzed with grief inside Pleasures. I would never see Mom's legs again. Her voice did loops in my mind. It was always there, underneath the stripper music, daring me to go on without her. *Fuck everyone*, I thought, flinging my bra onto the stage.

In the distance all I could see were the blurred heads, necks, and shoulders of men slumped in their seats as if they'd been sitting there for weeks, nursing pints of beer and watching us. Their defeated faces soothed me. I inhaled the familiar stench of peach Victoria's Secret peach body spray and Lysol and lowered myself to the ground onto my black stilettos like balancing on two ballpoint pens. The grubby red carpet seemed to spin beneath me as I walked towards the few clients. It was dead inside Pleasures but, angry as I was, I felt at home there.

Then I caught him looking at me. He was a pasty blonde, chubby kid in tan shorts and a baggy white T-shirt. He didn't look old enough to be at Pleasures. *He's got a fake ID.* He sipped clear liquid from a rocks glass and said he was from Long Beach.

"How'd you get here?" I said.

"Train." He showed me pictures of his two cats, told me about his mother's boyfriend, their arguments, and their pot smoking.

"Where's your dad?" I asked.

"Here in Pasadena." He said his name was Shawn and, tipsy, slid his arm around my shoulders. Onstage, an Asian girl with thigh-high boots and fake reading glasses gyrated to "Bold as Love" by Jimi Hendrix. I watched her spin expertly around the pole. My thighs stuck to the seat. I scooted closer to him and crossed my legs.

"I'm a virgin," he said.

"No, you're not." I squeezed his knee. I believed him.

"I really am." He was three vodka tonics brave. I imagined he ordered them because it seemed mature, like a drink Alec Baldwin would order in a romantic comedy.

"Can you show me?" he asked. "I'll pay you."

"Yes." It spilled out of my mouth before I could take it back. After a few more dances and a few more drinks Shawn was drunk. I gave him my phone number so we could set something up. He suggested we meet at my apartment where I would teach him how to kiss, show him how to fuck. And for this lesson, I'd be paid. It wasn't a lot of money, but this wasn't only about the money. It's about drying the dishes, emptying the garbage. It's about a childhood of digging through Mom's purse and chewing all of her skinny red sticks of Dentyne gum while we sang out loud to "The Tide is High" on the radio. It's about stomping through the last hospital when the power went out looking for warm sheets, a warm towel, enraged when I had to wait. *Fuck all of you*, I thought, with my arms crossed.

Mom raised me to believe I could do what I liked with my body. "Never feel like you have to have kids," she had said between drags of her More menthols, staring into the green light before lunging forward. I never felt like I did, and wondered if she felt trapped and pressured by having me. She hadn't raised me to sell my body for money, but she hadn't raised me not to sell my body for money either.

SHAWN SHOWED UP WITH his bicycle, which he carried up my stairs and leaned against the wall in the hallway. He handed me a sealed white envelope. I tore it open and counted the stiff bills. Three hundred. I felt silly in a dress with red and green cherries on it and wished I would have worn something more severe and authoritative. I led him to my couch and French kissed him deeply

"Like this," I said. The Black Keys played quietly in the background on NPR. I removed my bra and slid his hands along my bare hips. I kissed him for exactly three songs, and then I led him to my bedroom, where white tea-light candles burned softly. I tore open a condom and showed him how to put it on, careful not to seem like an airline attendant demonstrating a life vest. He was resting on clean white sheets, exactly like the ones on Mom's last hospital bed when she'd said, "no diapers" while she shivered and moaned. I fucked Shawn until I felt something and the thing I felt was fucked.

That afternoon, a giant bird-of-paradise outside my window reminded me of Mom's mighty rhubarb plant. It kept infiltrating her strawberries, no matter how many times she trimmed it back. Nothing could stop its spiky orange and purple blossoms, how it leaned into the afternoon sun, hungry for light.

Shawn couldn't come. He was nervous. Flesh was too scary. Squishy. Confrontational. "It's okay," I said and used my mouth and hand to stroke him until he was hard again.

He finally came with one hand on his cock and the other resting on my belly. Moments later, I sprung up and brought him a clean white towel signaling the end of our first lesson. "I'll make you a CD with rock music you'll like," he said. I gave him a tentative hug and he left. I locked my doors and turned up the radio. Loud. PJ Harvey sang on the radio in the other room. Little fish, big fish, swimming in the water, and I thought about all of us dancing in the cloudy, cracked mirrors at Pleasures, the daughters of mothers who taught us the value of a cheap underwire bra holding our 36Cs in place, and how to slide on our fishnet stockings so the seam climbed straight up our legs—how to smile when impossibly sad.

# 38

*P*ASADENA IS AFRAID OF nipples and their nipple phobia is how they succeeded closing down Pleasures when I stripped there. At first, they made us cover our nipples at all times, so we cut heart shapes from flowered wallpaper and glued them to our nipples before dancing onstage. A couple weeks later, they enforced the red line rule: we couldn't be topless beyond a line of red tape marking the legal yardage between our nipples and the customers seated at the stage. Finally, we couldn't take our tops off anywhere in the club—in effect making Pleasures a non-strip club. No longer could Marines, drug dealers, and felons enjoy the privilege of beer, shooting pool, eating an overcooked steak, and getting a table dance under one roof. They had to go to Vegas for that.

By the time Pasadena won their nipple war, Mom had been dead several months. I was at a loss for what to do. "Do you want some of my sensual massage clients?" Kara asked me. "It's the best blue-collar gig out there." Since Mom died, I couldn't get myself together to audition at any more clubs. The blinding migraines were back. I couldn't remember to buy toothpaste no matter how many times I wrote it on my hand with a black Sharpie. My socks didn't match. Kara showed me how to place some ads online in the adult services section and handed me some coconut oil. We set some appointments up.

After Dennis and Steve, one of the appointments I made was with a guy named Joe, who wanted to meet me in a hotel lobby in Little Tokyo. I was scrambling for rent, cat-sitter cash, and a little spending dough when Joe said, "Will you meet me for a drink in the lobby first?"

Be agreeable, never desperate, Kara had coached.

"Sure. I'll be wearing a black dress with a jacket."

At 9:20 P.M. I pulled into the parking lot of the lobby and walked in. I'd emailed Joe a picture so he had no problem recognizing me. A tall Latino man wearing a black motorcycle jacket waved me over to a table where he sat in front of a green bottle of beer and a dish full of wasabi peas. He was thirty-something. He reached in with thick fingers and popped two in his mouth.

"Want one?" He swished the last of his Becks around in the bottle before swallowing the final sip.

"No, thanks." Everything about Joe was thick.

"I'm married," he held up his giant hand to show me his ring. I shrugged.

"Lots of people are," I said.

"This could be a regular thing," he said.

"Great." His cell phone sat on the table in front of him. He glanced at it. I did too.

"So, you do fetishes?" He asked.

"I have some clients who enjoy that. I have a lot of equipment: ropes, cuffs, titty-clamps, a blow-up butt plug—you name it," I said. I wished he would've hinted he wanted kink when he called.

"I don't want anything up my butt." This was supposed to make me laugh, so I chuckled and instantly regretted calling Joe a couple of times to confirm—something I never ever do. Never chase a client down. Always be the one chased.

"Okay. Nothing up your butt." I looked around for a clock but didn't see one. My phone was in my purse. He was probably one of those guys who resented hiring women so he wanted to fuck with me and make wise cracks. A time waster.

"So, you're going to give me a massage?"

"Mmhmm," I said.

"And you're going to give me a handjob?"

"Yeah."

"I have two hundred for you, but there's more for the taking."

"Okay." More meant more time, which meant we should hurry so I could make another appointment downtown.

"Shall we get out of here?" I asked.

"Let's do that."

Outside, in the parking lot, there were two guys hanging out in front of a van. One was bald and the other was short with lots of brown curly hair and glasses.

"These guys want to talk to you," Joe said.

"What?"

The bald guy told me to turn around, then cuffed me and shoved me in the back of a van. "Is this real?" I asked. He showed me the badge pinned to his chest. "This is real."

# 39

"ARE YOU A PROSTITUTE?" A beautiful, Latina with long straight hair in a single ponytail asked me. Her brown eyes glowed in the dull, cramped holding cell. She reminded me of girls I stripped with back in SF when I was a bald, lesbian, feminist with a pierced septum, ready to take down the patriarchy with my boring, self-righteous anger. This girl was barely eighteen.

"Do I look like a prostitute?" I was sitting on a metal bench, squished between two women, knee to knee.

"There are five black women, a Hispanic woman, and you. You're a prostitute," she said. She turned around, hopped up on a ledge, and looked out the tiny window, then back to me. I nodded.

"Why are you a prostitute?" she asked. Her voice just above a whisper. I chewed my lip. Looked up at her.

"That's a good question," I said. If she were Andrea Dworkin, she would accuse me of being a brainwashed drone of the patriarchy, succumbing to the violence against women. But I'd never thought of myself as a prostitute. *Until now.*

I'd never been a streetwalker or even a call girl; never worked for an agency or Madame. I'd made a choice in my early twenties. Unlike many young women, I wasn't forced by a pimp. I hadn't been sold into sex slavery by my family. I had chosen to fuck once or twice for money—but had also chosen to stop. I'd scaled back to handjobs only. So I didn't feel deserving of that label. Sex worker, yes. Prostitute, no.

*Was there a difference?* I remember thinking, *If I smoked crack a couple times, does that make me a crackhead?* But crackheads are helpless. I was not helpless.

Until now.

The girl looked sorry for me, or disgusted. She shrugged and looked away.

There was a loud buzz. The door was released. A muscular butch with one very long braid walked in and hugged my gorgeous Latina cellmate. They kissed and the cell began to heat up. The lovers had been in a bar fight and were covered in pepper spray.

My throat itched. The rest of the women coughed and put their heads between their knees for air. One drunk girl squatted on the toilet and threw a used Maxi pad across the cell. She laughed as it hit the wall and slid down.

The black girls who were busted for prostitution told me to request O.R. This meant I'd never been arrested before and could perhaps be released without bail. They settled in, knew the ropes, and followed procedure. One made a call for me to ask about my release.

"You shouldn't be here," she said. "They may keep you all weekend." She rested her head on my lap and feel asleep.

Hours later, we were escorted upstairs and told to stand against a wall. The light was a dead yellow. We were handed scratchy blankets, which were more like tarps. The jailers snatched my black tights and stuck them in a Ziploc bag, to prevent me from strangling myself with them. I was buzzed into another cell where a woman was asleep in the lower bunk. Her clear stripper shoes—exactly like ones I owned and danced in—were on the floor below her.

I climbed onto the top bunk where, on the wall, someone had scribbled the words "I love you, Mom."

*Fuck.* Of course I get the bunk where someone scratched "I love you, Mom" in glitter nail polish. Why couldn't I have gotten dad? Or just a pimp's name like "I love Rico My Baby Daddy Forever." No, it said Mom, and now I had no choice but to sit here and think about her. I wanted my mother. She had been dead for a year.

The only light was through a mail-like slot that looked into the center of a room. All I could see was a pay phone and women in line for showers. Over a loudspeaker, names were called for court, but not mine. I heard other sounds: the yelling, buzzing, coughing, and lights snapping on and off. No way could I sleep here. I bolted up and went to the door. Pounded against it. I found a buzzer above the toilet. I held my fist on it. My breaths were shallow.

"Guess you're staying all weekend too," my cellmate said from her bunk.

"No," I said. I sunk down near her dirty stripper shoes, ashamed at what I had become. Helpless.

# 40

"STOP RINGING THE BELL or I'll leave you in there all weekend," a jailer barked over the loud speaker. I laid on my back. It felt like hours were passing. I focused hard on the shimmer-scratched words. The word "Mom" left a taste of ashes and vanilla in my throat, and I wanted to call her. Who could I call? My breaths were short and tight. I mouthed the written words with the taste of her ashes in my throat, like a prayer. Unable to sleep, I breathed in the vanilla sweat from my jacket armpits—echoes of Mom's rice pudding smells haunted me.

Breakfast was dropped through the mail slot as if I were a stray dog. I felt like one as I nibbled a sausage patty, then I fell asleep briefly under my jacket. My answering machine dreams were back: Mom's voice talking about a detour ahead. "You've made a wrong turn, honey. Turn left up ahead. Would you just look at this spaghetti squash?"

The woman below me stirred. "Fuck, fuck," she said. It slowly sunk in. My cats weren't going to be fed. My car was going to be towed. My rent was going to be late, and I was in a cage.

I thought about my brother, who had been in and out of jail for petty theft. We wrote letters when he was in San Quentin. I had my brother's back when he was in jail. He got degrees in jail. He cooked and fought fires. Mom sent packages with socks and money for cigarettes, but she was still saddened and disappointed by Alan.

I didn't want to disappoint her, but I knew that I was. This was the tipping point I was afraid of—the serious fucking-up my life part. A series of bad turns until I was lost, never to return. In this cage, I was subhuman: lower than an animal because animals ate drank, slept, and shit. I did none of those things. Hours later, we were led to another cell with a bunch of concrete benches. The jail guard pointed to a woman who was busted for smoking weed in her car. "You have a visit." Then she looked at me. "You do, too."

"What?" I said, feeling stupid.

The jailer gave me a stern, annoyed look, and talked slow as if I was a retarded monkey. "You. Have. A. Visit."

I followed the woman who had smoked weed in her car and stood, waiting in line. When I got to the window, it was Kara. I put my hand on the glass on top of hers and cried.

"I'm going to get you out of here," she said. My tongue was so dry I couldn't speak. "You don't belong in here." She laughed gently. Shook her head. "You're the most innocent prostitute."

After a while I said, "I thought they got you, too." I was led back to the concrete cell with the others and covered myself with a scratchy gray blanket, waiting in the dark. One girl was passed out on the floor, but most of the women sat with their knees up on the cool cement bench, waiting.

I must've dozed off because I heard the same jailer yell, "You're O.R." I was sticky, smelly, hungry, tired, and ashamed, but I knew what those letters meant, and they meant I was free.

Back in my apartment, the cats were loud and hungry. I removed all my sensual massage ads from the Internet. T-Mobile threatened to shut off my phone in twenty-four hours without two hundred bucks, and I was in shock—too scared to book any more clients. My apartment was in disarray. I received hurt and angry emails from the client I was supposed to meet me later on that night—a finance man from Palm Beach. Kara was spooked as well. We had been doing sensual massage jobs together and hadn't feared the cops. We figured there was enough violent crime in Los Angeles to busy the police. We thought wrong. I'd heard from a sober junkie who used to rob banks say that, "Once you get arrested, you keep getting arrested." I couldn't break my mom's heart the way my brother did. My brother, who was dumb enough to hold up our favorite corn dog shack, Fresh Freeze, where we rode our bikes as kids and sat at the picnic tables outside and sipped chocolate milkshakes and nibbled fish sandwiches with way too much mayo. He got three years for his troubles. I didn't want to ruin my life with a misdemeanor for prostitution on my record. I couldn't do that to her again. Even dead, I wouldn't do that to her.

Then again, it was a tribe of sex workers who had helped me survive, by showing me how to make phone calls and being kind to me; explaining that I could be released O.R. and that I had no business being in jail— no business at all.

# 41

*I* FELL APART; SO DID my shit brown Nova. Broke
down right in front of Cheetahs on Hollywood
Boulevard, where I was making about a hundred
bucks a night with punk, hipster strippers—girls with
an edgy, fetish look. The economy was in bad shape
and getting worse, and I saw it tire the eyes of the
customers at the bar. They'd suckle a Budweiser for
an hour, rest their chins on their fists, and watch the
Lakers on the television screen above the Ms. Pac-Man
video game. Financial tension made the girls cranky.
They'd strut from table to table, glaring at each other
while competing for the two customers at the bar. One
guy, Larry, never bought dances unless he fell in love
with a girl and got her drunk. She had to promise to
date him, and if she did he would give her six hundred
bucks a night. Another guy, a Russian thug, only liked
young, skinny blonde girls with flat chests. As a thick,

non-drinking redhead with muscular thighs and tattoos, I didn't have a chance. Cheetahs was dead, but we still had to be dressed and on the floor by seven. Dressed— meaning in our underwear. A leggy girl with a Mohawk got up from a card game and pressed her cheek against our floor manager's hairy chest.

"We're starving, Vinny. Get us a pizza."

He mumbled something about piranhas and walked away. Her desperation cracked the veneer of her tight Hollywood smile. She clung to a little Hello Kitty purse that held blow and lint.

Cheetahs reflected my ugly loneliness back to me and I couldn't stay away from it. I'd say anything for twenty-five bucks. Instead of selling dances, I sold loneliness, got them smitten. Made empty promises, gave them my phone number, told them I'd meet them for dinner, play tennis with them, go to Vegas, Mexico. "I'll kill you if you don't marry me," one guy said. I told him I would.

Stripping wasn't always this emotionally complicated.

Part of the problem in L.A. is the rules that separate booze from touching. Local and state laws change every few years regarding nudity and physical contact in the clubs. Where there's alcohol, there's no contact. When Willy Brown was mayor up in San Francisco in the nineties, full contact lap dancing was legal. We paid a stage fee, and dot-com money flowed. Now, in L.A., topless clubs weren't even topless anymore. Touching was a misdemeanor and owners feared losing their businesses.

Which is why I got called into the manager's office.

"Why do you let them touch you?" Vinny asked. He pointed at the monitor.

"How do you know that guy's not undercover? You want to get us raided? You want to do more, go to the Bunny Ranch in Vegas."

My knee rubbed a customer's inner thigh. I let him grab my hips. My hair poured into his face. My lips touched his neck.

My days were numbered.

I got a text from Christine, a friend who was dancing in New Orleans: you should come work at Visions. It's good here.

It took one text to extract me from the claws of lady Los Angeles—I bought a one way ticket to where I could be groped without being fired.

On the way to the airport, I played Mom's old messages over and over: "You've got to get that degree. Just stay in grad school. If I were your age and not married, I'd stay in school the rest of my life."

I could do my schoolwork from New Orleans. The thing about writing is you can do it anywhere.

# 42

WHEN YOU FALL YOU have to land, preferably somewhere dimly lit and topless, where funny money is tossed like glitter and there is full contact lap dancing, loose rules, and lots of tourism. I flew to New Orleans with twelve bucks in my pocket. I wasn't going to get arrested dancing topless on Bourbon Street. "The weather's ninety degrees with ninety percent humidity," the stewardess announced on the plane. People moaned, but I was ready to be wrapped in southern steam. Out of the airport, I was hit by heat. New Orleans is a sweaty pussy that sticks to your face, soaks into your skin, and stays the night.

"Visions," I said. Like hairdressers and keepers of the occult codes in New Orleans, the cab driver knew where to go.

Visions is twenty minutes from the airport, nowhere near the frenzy of Bourbon Street. The only things that far off Downman are some railroad tracks, a Domino's Pizza, and a condemned liquor store. There are no billboards advertising Visions, just a sign on the building that reads, "Visions: where the locals go."

From the outside, Visions looked like a gutted Denny's. A wire fence held back weeds and ivy, but the vines pushed through the fence, crashing to the gravel below. A truck parked in the lot had a bumper sticker: "Nawlins. Proud to swim home."

I stepped out of the cab with my rolling suitcase, duffel bag and computer, sticky from the air. Live oaks reached across the sky and dangled curvy shadows across the street. The rain suddenly stopped, and the sun seared through the mist. I walked up cement stairs and entered. It was dark as hell: a smoky dungeon promising spiders, tits, and beer.

My friend Christine worked here but not that night, so I had no pull. "Talk to the night manager, Rick," she'd said. "He's the nice guy."

"I'm here to see Rick, to audition," I said to a thin, pale guy with a big head and a limp. He crossed his arms and eyeballed my suitcase.

"He's not here. And it's Friday night so you can't get on the schedule."

I figured I wasn't going to get hired: I was too fat, too old, and too tattooed. Still, he hesitated.

"Wait at the bar," he said.

I rolled my luggage to a stool and watched the day shift girls change into the night shift.

In the dark heat, I knew this was my world: a smoky place where the lonely hide and tough girls jiggle their butts. I dialed Mom's number to hear her voice on the machine for luck, but the club was too loud. I could barely hear her cheery hello. The topless girls dancing on the bar wore g-strings that were more like strategically placed threads. Meaty thighs wiggled to the rhythm of Jimmie Vaughan's "Can't Say No." The rule was that guys had to tip if they sat at the bar, and they had to be drinking or they'd be asked to leave. A recorded male voice said so every few minutes, to remind customers and discourage squatters.

I was relieved to see the range of body types and the signature dead gazes come from girls floating on plastic heels. They were real girls with round hips, stretch marks and crooked smiles; their garters held stacks of green. They were making money. Maybe I could, too.

An hour passed. I was tired from the flight. My outfit wasn't sexy, and I had nowhere to stay. Christine was at Jazz Fest, not answering her phone.

The limper paced the club with his smirk. Guys like him have the power to reject the beautiful girls they couldn't touch in high school. Managers of strip clubs were always cartoon versions of themselves, and I was a faded, tired version of myself.

Rick showed after all. He had the bleakness that only guys whose days begin and end in strip clubs understand. He waved me into an office the size of a bathtub where both managers stood in the dark.

"How'd you find out about this place?" Rick asked. There was a cash machine counting bills. It stopped at a hundred. It was loud as a hair dryer.

"Christine told me."

"Show me your body." I lifted up my shirt and removed my bra; pulled down my pants to my knees. He ran one hand over his greasy silver hair, and with the other he grabbed my ass and held it, sampling the flab there. It was ample.

"Are there any more tattoos or just your arms?"

"Just my arms."

"You need day girls?" Rick asked the limper.

"Naaah." The limper shuffled papers. His eyes glowed in the shadows. The cash machine spat out bills. Red lights showed digital numbers and a click-click-click of plastic heels announced a blonde stripper, puffing on a cigarette. My eyes burned.

"Go downtown. Try Bourbon," he said. They loved their hazing routine and were delighted to reject me. Nice guy Rick stuck a rubber band over a wad of cash. I pushed my boobs together and tilted my head to the side, begging. I had to convince them of my earning abilities. I needed one night shift to prove myself, but they didn't care if I'd come from sucking off Hugh Hefner at the Playboy Mansion, they didn't want me at Visions. I pulled up my jeans and fastened my bra. The limper laughed and shook his head. Rick checked his watch. My audition was over.

"Stick around for an hour and if I need girls, you can stay," he said. I rolled my suitcase into the dressing room where naked girls barked into cell phones, slammed metal lockers, applied mascara, and smoked cigarettes. A drunk girl with black Cleopatra bangs collapsed on the floor. Her eyeballs rolled back in her head.

"My brother's dead. Is my brother dead?" she said. A tiny redhead in a plaid skirt held her by the waist. "You've got to go home, sweetie," she said to the girl, who tried to stand but slid back down to the floor instead.

Rick appeared and walked over.

"Get dressed. You're going home." He reached in his back pocket for bolt cutters and opened her locker.

"My brother. Is he dead?" She stuck to the wall and didn't let go.

The plaid skirt girl looked at me.

"Hand me her stuff." I reached up to locker twenty-nine and grabbed her clothes.

There's an unspoken bond among strippers. No matter what happened, if a dancer's in trouble, the girls help, or mind their own business—whatever is needed.

We dressed her and called a cab. The other strippers went back to their glitter, body spray, lip gloss voodoo. I shoved my bag into locker twenty-nine and knew I'd found my tribe: a pirate society that understood itself. We were there for a singular purpose. If pressed, it was us against the world. Rick put the bolt cutters back in his pocket and turned to me. He said, "Welcome to Visions."

On the main floor, the cowboy sized me up like I was livestock.

"How old are you, sweetheart?"

"How old do you think?"

He held my jaw in his scratchy palm and moved it around to check my profile.

"Well, you're not nineteen." He crossed his arms over his belly that bounced as he laughed. "Most the girls here are twenty-three." He stared hard at my face for an indication of my fossil stripper status.

"And most of them are lying to you," I said. Most of them had husbands or boyfriends, three kids at home with a sitter, and had danced on this very bar for ten years. They had wrinkles, an eighth-grade education, and crooked teeth, which is exactly what I loved about Visions—it was the creamed corn of strip clubs, and I fit in. I looked country, as long as I covered my tattoos and shut my mouth about my post-graduate studies.

The cowboy guzzled a Bud Light and squinted at me through smoke. I was teetering towards geriatric stripper, and I wondered if he knew it. I grinned at him anyway, because after a couple drinks he wouldn't give a shit. He'd get a few dances, and I'd leave with a stack of twenties.

"You'd be correct in guessing I'm not nineteen," I sassed, sipping a Diet Coke. "I just turned thirty-three, and am fast approaching my sexual prime. You should invest now while you still have a chance." I slapped my ass to punctuate. *I could really do with about five hundred bucks.*

*How old are you?* The age stigma didn't apply to guys—a thing that made me want to pour my Diet Coke on his lap, instead of grind on it. His cigar smoke surrounded us when I moved close enough to see his face. He could've been anywhere between forty and fifty-five. Southern men age faster than California men. They eat fried catfish and pralines, skip gym memberships and go fishing. They smoke nonstop, which adds lines to their fat faces. I eyeball a biscuit and my thighs expand. I smell a cupcake and it adds an inch to my middle. Next time around, I want to be a tall, skinny man with the metabolism of a whippet. My mom, the expert baker, taught me how to worship sugar. I begged to lick her cookie dough bowls the minute I could talk. I couldn't shovel sugar into my mouth fast enough.

When her body shriveled from the first cancer, I started running on the treadmill. The treadmill was the place my rage could pummel the ground without hurting anyone. I ran from cancer.

"How many kids you got?" asked the cowboy.

"None." I shook my head. Time felt like peanut butter in Visions. I played like I was relaxed and just hung out while mentally counting songs and strategizing the best moment to bring up business. This wasn't it.

I'd wait until he finished Bud Light number two. Zoey was onstage. A skinny blonde thing in pigtails, knee socks, and a white skirt. She danced to Bonnie Raitt. Unlike the clubs on Bourbon Street that insisted on upbeat top forty bullshit, like Kings of Leon and Lady fucking Gaga, we could play whatever music we wanted at Visions. At Visions, we got to be edgy. I stripped to everything from Skinny Puppy to Ike Turner. The cowboy gulped down a second beer.

"You eat Zapp's potato chips?" he asked.

"Why? Do I smell like onion dip?"

He chuckled. One of his arms wrapped around my hip.

"I guess it's your lucky night," he said. It certainly was. Considering the quality of conversation and the fact that I didn't have a shotgun within reach, it was a lucky night for both of us.

"I think they have some of those chips in the vending machine. You want some?"

I glanced across the room. Next to the poker slots, where two men chain-smoked, the vending machine was sitting swathed in yellow-green light.

"No need. You're looking at the creator of Zapp's potato chips." He puffed up his chest like a rooster.

"No kidding," I grinned wide and squelched an impulse to smash his beer bottle into my forehead. "Well, Mister Zapp, let's get better acquainted." I pointed to the VIP lap dancing area, where I could finally extract some dough. "I just got married, and I love pussy," he said. Strutting like a rooster he followed me into the room where I straddled him and offered my boobs like M&M's for his open mouth.

"You should move into my trailer," he offered. I considered this proposal carefully, imagining a grubby trailer with gingham curtains lodged in a marsh.

"Does it have Wi-Fi?"

Christine let me crash at her place in Algiers Point that she rented from a redheaded bartender at a famous bar on Bourbon Street. She introduced me to the redhead's family, and I ended up renting the place by the week while she stayed at her boyfriend's place uptown. Her pad not only had Wi-Fi but a Chi Machine: a funny plastic machine that plugged into the wall and wiggled my ankles for a timed five minutes. Mom would've loved the Chi Machine. It was hypnotic, relaxing, and soothing for my lower back. My body may have wanted to be fat but, like any retirement-aged athlete, I followed a strict diet and exercise regime that involved lifting weights and soaking in bags upon bags of Epsom salts, while depriving myself of sugar. I thought about Mr. Zapp barging into the place and expecting payment worthy of rent. "I've got a place already."

I stood on the sticky red vinyl couch riddled with holes from spiked heels, my pussy inches from the cowboy's face. His loneliness collided with mine. It made me sick but felt like the best thing in the world.

He was the first in a string of big southern kahunas that talked to me about their jobs and golf games, tweaked my nipples, tried to stick their fingers in my pussy, and spent hundreds of dollars on my body. Every night I danced at Visions, I cleared anywhere from three hundred to a thousand bucks. The better I got at hustling dances, the more I noticed my boundaries slide. I made customers think I was invested in them, that I was accessible. And I was. That part of me that allowed them to get smitten for twenty minutes or an hour was happy and free. Sometimes, I let them camp out inside the hole Mom left. But after they left Visions I made them disappear by dialing my answering machine, listening for the comfort of her voice: "They're trying to kill me. I have to get out of here. You should come get me out of here."

In Algiers, I ran along the levy—the one that didn't burst during Katrina, while cicadas buzzed in the river. The humidity was heavy and hot. My pace slowed but, dripping with sweat, I watched boats gliding on the surface of the Mississippi knowing Mom would've loved Algiers Point.

# 43

WHEN I OPENED LOCKER twenty-nine at 5:00 P.M., it was sweltering in the dressing room. I peeled off my damp jeans in favor of a light blue skirt that wasn't really a skirt—more of a faded doily with loose threads. I stood in front of a big silver fan that blew dust on my greasy face. It was my third consecutive night working at Visions. My thighs burned from over use. At forty years old, my stripper days had been numbered for ten years. Now, making more money than ever, I felt like the Brett Favre of strippers: injured and aging out, but reluctant to retire. My winning streak could change on a dime.

Stripper Fog is like a hangover without drugs or alcohol. The few hours of sleep you get have no effect because it's the sleep that happens between 4:00 A.M. and noon. It's a full-body ache, a stiff neck, and a headache that no amount of ibuprofen or coffee can remedy. On

Stripper Fog days I'm up until sunrise; I pull the curtains shut and count my money—separate out the cash that goes to pay rent and bills into Ziploc bags to hide in a secret compartment inside my suitcase. I shower to calm the buzz, then crash like the tail end of a speed bender. I don't reach for Xanax anymore to get quality shut eye, even though I want to. When I wake up the sunlight's so bright I feel like my eyes will explode. I approach migraine territory when I'm run down—I get them more easily. My boobs sore from high impact fondling, I smear a thick salve of greasy medicinal homeopathic goo on them until they stick to the inside of my T-shirt. The gel removes bruises and heals nipples chafed by whiskered chins. I have razor burn on my crotch from shaving it every single day.

The recovery time is longer than it used to be. Stripper Fog requires rehydration and rest; gallons of water and thousands of milligrams of vitamin C. I soak in Epsom salts until the water runs cold, soothing the speedball of Diet Coke, sugar free Red Bull, and Excedrin PM. My knees have bruises the size of poker chips from crawling on a wooden stage for eight hours. My lower back aches, a recent development. It's from bending over in six-inch heels at an unnatural angle so frat boys from Alabama can stick dollar bills in my garter. The angle bends my hips forward, and after hours of dancing it hurts to bend over. And then it hurts to sit down. Finally, it hurts to lie down and sleep. *I'm going to miss this*, I think. In a few hours I'll head back to Visions in the backseat of a taxi towards Downman Road, even though it's hell to turn my neck, and there's shooting pain from my shoulder to my elbow from swinging around the pole by one arm. I will hold a large iced coffee from Café Beignet and balance my bulky pink bag of costumes between my knees and wonder how much longer I can do this.

By the time I walked into Visions, the sun had dropped and the heavy wet air glued my t-shirt to my sweaty stomach. In the locker room, I grabbed baby wipes for a quick bath and, having forgotten a towel, I ripped scratchy brown paper towels from the dispenser over the sink and dried off.

"Hey, it's that bitch with that hair." Chloe, a local stripper with a cigarette in one hand and a Miller in the other slammed her locker beside me. Between her country Louisiana accent and her drunkenness, I barely understood her, but was happy to see her. "How's it out there today?" I asked. She was bowlegged and pretty in the face with defined cheekbones and a tough, sarcastic smile.

"I don't know about this luau," she said. "They're drunk but they're not spending."

"The worst kind of crowd," I said. She mumbled something and walked back out onto the floor. New Orleans was dead in the summertime. It was also hurricane season, so to encourage business Visions hosted a luau—a Hawaiian meal-cum-feast.

I shoved a turquoise flower comb in my hair and prepared to throw my legs over my head and dance for the next seven hours. Visions had a skanky reputation, but it was my favorite club by far—my tried and true safe haven. I was never expected to touch dick or asked to by customers, even though people assumed that was the norm. Visions was a locals-only titty bar, and its sleaze factor worked in our favor. I walked out onto the floor like I was grateful to own the place and surveyed the land. Chloe tipped her beer in my direction and I became that bitch with that hair among the pulled pork, cheese cubes, and jambalaya on platters on top of the pool tables—buffet style for the luau.

All three bartenders were working, and the bar was packed with local dudes drinking a scary pink half-price rum drink, which explained why my shoes stuck to the floor when I walked over to the pool tables. I popped three purple grapes into my mouth, watching two customers eat cubes of cheese off a cocktail napkin and play the slots. I checked in with Eddie, my favorite DJ who was always quitting smoking. He was playing "Just Like Putty" by Jimmie Vaughan and chomping Big Red gum.

"You quit again?"

"And how," he said. "Candy, you're up in three girls."

"I'm feeling The Black Keys and Zeppelin," I said, studying the potential classic rock diehards in the crowd. He knew this meant "Lies" and "Whole Lotta Love." During my seven-minute set, Zeppelin fans walked up to the stage and tossed dollars in the air, heads knodding in sync to the rhythm. The stage was slick, and my heels were ground to the metal tips—like dancing on two ballpoint pens. A tall white guy wearing a baseball cap walked up to me. I noticed he preferred the older chicks, like the curvy black girl named Promise who's in nursing school and wore no makeup, and Marianne, a tall, thin girl with crazy black mermaid hair and three kids. The nurse frowned at me when Dennis talked to me, but I always smiled at her. I knew I must watch myself with the local girls—play extra nice and help them out once in a while, or they could fuck up my hustle by talking shit about me. I'd seen them shun outsiders and considered myself lucky to have slipped beneath their locals-only radar. Management told me I couldn't work on Thursday nights because only the local girls could get on the schedule that night.

On stage, I kept my gaze on the baseball cap guy. He grinned with his whole head. His tiny bright blue eyes stared out behind thick glasses. I squatted for dollars with my feet on either side of his head with my heels on his shoulders, then pushed my pelvis up towards the ceiling. Too exhausted to do more pole tricks, I cat-crawled on the wooden stage. When I glanced at the TV screens above the bar, I noticed the Saints were winning again, and the customers at Visions were ecstatic about it. An electrical current of euphoria buzzed. The Saints were rebuilding their spirit as I was rebuilding mine. I winced from the shooting pain in my neck and realized that I liked to swing around the pole and float upside down because floating was easier than landing. When I was onstage, I got a rush of happiness and monumental relief from knowing men desired me—knowing that I was desirable. I realize this was childish. It wasn't the real world, but it was the world I was in longer than any other.

"I'm Dan," the guy said. Dan waited for me by the stage while I dashed into the manager's office and popped three Advil, then made the required rounds dancing on top of the bar.

A tall, curvy blonde who always danced to Michael Jackson and Madonna wore a black flower in her hair and a white, oversized men's dress shirt was dancing in front of me. She had a devious smile and great, thick legs. She did this thing with her boobs where she flexed her pectoral muscles and her boobs bounced one at a time. I followed her along the bar where we had to dance in front of every guy, which could take about twenty-five minutes, and if every guy tipped one or two bucks, we could make about eighty bucks right away. I liked to use stage time as a way to hook guys—flirt and coax them into a lap dance for the real money. That night, I was annoyed that I had to follow the blonde. She took her time. She was drunk. She was chatting and crouching in front of every single guy. She was taking forever. And she was doing her boob thing. I was pissed, and I was going to do something to get her to make a move.

I reached over and felt her tit with my right hand and smiled at the guy in front of her. "I've never made out with you," she said to me, bewildered and ignoring the customers. I kissed her for a while, tongue and all. She tasted like sweet alcohol, which was unusual for me. The guys at the bar in front of us held out more than a few singles. We moved onto the next guys to do our kissing routine.

The blonde could kiss. I hadn't been kissed in a while. I hadn't realized how insanely lonely I was: devastated, furiously alone. I would've kissed a gator. The blonde pointed to the guys in front of us. "Not them, they're too country," she said. I trusted her local instincts and danced for them on my own, grabbed the bars above me for balance and twirled around, bent over at my waist. When bent in half, I could touch the bar with my palms. A customer's hand touched my calf. Where else was I going to walk away with five or six hundred bucks on a Friday night? Where else were strangers going to tell me I'm intelligent and wonderful? How will I do anything else?

NEW ORLEANS SHOWED ME how to do death. During Mardi Gras, locals dressed their dead up like a parade and marched through the streets, clapped hands, and danced wildly, covered in feathers and beads. I needed to jump into the arms of Death and celebrate the cycle of life. I walked graveyards and offered glitter nail polish to Marie Laveau. I needed a miracle to sew me up so I walked among the dead—the washed up hillbilly bones in graveyards of the poor. In New Orleans, death was an elaborate pageant that caused people to hop up and blow horns. Marching bands and Mardi Gras Indians came out into the streets, and I lunged into the middle of it.

Mardi Gras was gray and misty in New Orleans. I walked to the French Quarter to meet up with friends who were Mardi Gras pros. By 3:00 P.M. the streets were frantic with marching bands and thousands of drunks in silly hats. They screamed at each other on balconies—threw green, purple, and gold sparkling beads. It was a mob scene of hot dog stands and plastic cups, including police roaming around perched atop their horses, surveying the crowd. They're only decoration, really, there's no order during Mardi Gras and all bets are off. On the ground, beads covered Bourbon Street and gathered in mud puddles right in front of The Bruiser, my next place of employment.

I surrendered to the mob scene. Dove in, clutched my wallet, and was carried into work by the crowd.

MY SOUL BELONGED IN New Orleans, but the rest of me missed California. If I ever wanted to go back, I had to complete a diversion program to get the arrest stricken from my record. After a month of dancing, I longed for home: ripe oranges and figs from the trees in my backyard, organic cherry tomatoes, fresh squeezed carrot juice, and wheat grass shots in the cafés in my neighborhood. Besides, California was my mom. I sensed her tucked inside the branches of redwoods like the fog. What was the other option? Move full time to New Orleans and be a forty-year-old stripper? I couldn't leave California entirely—I couldn't leave Mom behind. I was still in grad school and was writing papers, preparing a lecture, and completing my book-length manuscript on my days off. I promised her I'd finish grad school and had six months until graduation. I needed to get back to class for my upcoming residency. I missed my one-bedroom apartment in Silver Lake, with the monstrous avocado tree that tore up the sidewalk—its powerful roots shifted the ground beneath me, reminding me of earthquakes.

I read Faulkner, Lorrie Moore, and Mary Gaitskill. I learned that a comma goes inside the quotation marks. I learned that tension on the page is two people saying "No." I devoured stories by Barry Hannah, Steve Almond, and Richard Yates. I was directed to vary my sentence structure. I studied with professors whose direction and input became deeply influential—not only in writing, but in life. They made a living reading stories and writing books, while I was having a stare down with forty—and dancing topless in New Orleans to pay rent in Los Angeles.

I packed a bag and flew back home, knowing I could skate a while on the dough I'd made in New Orleans, and knowing as long as I had enough for a flight back, I could make more.

# 44

*I* HAD AN 11:00 A.M. appointment with the Alternative Justice Program back in L.A., which is how I could avoid jail time and a record. I needed to run on dirt. The sun was already white-hot by 8:00 A.M. The light skipped across the water while lazy ducks floated around on the surface. On my run, I cooed at toddlers on jungle gyms and watched yoga moms with glorious ponytails stretch on mats in a bright yellow room. A man about thirty-five held a baby, walked, and talked on the phone. I wondered what that's like, to have a baby, and wondered if I missed out on that possibility.

My knees and hips made morning clicking noises as I warmed up. Lap number one was like the first cup of coffee. By the second lap, "good morning" blurted out of my mouth to everyone that passed by. The rain had just stopped after several days of downpour, so there were lots of runners out. I dodged brown puddles and mud.

I know how lucky I am. Years ago, when I worked at the law firm in Century City, during my endless commute, I used to stare at morning runners with envy. *I'd give anything to be able to get up and run every day,* I had thought.

I met with my young, Jewish lawyer in his office downtown. "You're pulling on Superman's cape," he said. He asked me to stop writing about sex work until I completed the diversion program. I didn't want to pull on Superman's cape. I wanted to twist his balls off and eat them with gluten free pasta. I wanted to scream, "Fuck you, LAPD." But I didn't want to return to jail where an eighteen-year-old girl sat twitching on my lap saying, "My daddy's in here, too, my dude is busted," and, "I've been ho'ing since twelve." I remembered the Latina woman on the toilet pulling a dirty pad out of her underwear and tossing it in the corner. All the voices chanting, "Are we going to court? Are we going to court?" Jail smelled like a kennel. Questions were thrown at me, "Why are you a prostitute?" The guard yelled, "You're staying the weekend. Push that buzzer again and I'll leave you in there."

I pulled into the parking lot. My ads were no longer online, but I still had clients. I noticed an attendant directing a car out of a tight space. He didn't hand the driver an orange ticket or collect any money. My phone rang. I was eight minutes late but answered it anyway.

A woman with a thick nasal Hispanic accent asked me, "Do you do couples? Are you available right now?" and "I'm a transsexual. Do you have a problem with that?" I could smell the meth through the phone. I'd never done a session with a tranny before and no, I didn't have a problem with that, but I smelled trouble. I felt trouble in my belly. "I'm not available right now. I have a screening process before we meet. Maybe we can talk tomorrow." I knew the person on the other end of my phone wouldn't jump through my security hoops.

Twelve minutes late, I walked into a dark lobby and into a moldy elevator. *How does an elevator mold?* I found the right door where a note was posted that read: "Back in five minutes. Please wait" in Spanish and English. A Latina woman showed up with a trolly full of boxes. "We're moving files from a storage unit," she said. I walked into the office, watching her carry the boxes into the office, then slide them onto the floor. I picked up a magazine and sat down. "I have to go to the restroom, so I have to lock the door," she said. I didn't move.

"You can't be in here," she said, annoyed with me. I was a criminal to her. A prostitute. A waste of time. An animal. I was paperwork to her. More files in more boxes to store and unload. I walked back into the hallway and waited for her return.

"You can come in now," she said.

She wrote me a receipt, peeling my pink copy from her pad. Her handwriting was pretty and loopy, like my mom's. Anyone with penmanship that stunning should get the job, no matter how many times she left the "Back in five minutes" sign on her door.

She didn't ask me one question about my case, but complimented my black leather ankle boots. I forked over the fine: three hundred fifty-five bucks, most of which I borrowed from a friend. She handed me the paperwork.

"Take care," she said, without looking up.

Three fifty awarded me a DVD and workbook for a class called "Think About It," which was a take home, forty-page, multiple choice, third grade reading level workbook containing questions like: How to avoid violent behavior? Answer: Take an exercise class or go running. Don't pick up a pillow or take up boxing.

I refused to see clients unless I had seen them a few times already. I only had a couple happy ending regulars who called me once a month. I clenched my teeth and applied for a job at a juice bar. I wondered what it would take to quit this life. I was afraid that the detour I'd chosen would affect my life forever. I remembered, when I started stripping, hands crawled across my body like crabs and thick calloused fingers slipped beneath my g-string. I needed the money. I was in love with my speed dealer girlfriend. Sometimes I cried. It's never just about the money. I watched the other girls perform onstage in a way that appeared powerful and sexy, like they had emotional shellac that enabled them to shake off systematic rejection from men. I was snorting a quarter of meth a day and needed fast money so I learned how to mute my emotions—no one wants a topless dance from a crying stripper. I climbed from man to man no matter how I felt. There were come stains on my costumes, filthy fingers on my boobs, and beer breath in my face.

Sometimes I wish I had made a different choice when I was broke and feisty and alone. But I didn't. I became the hardest working dancer I could be. I learned how to extract blood from stone. I learned how to shut off. I put down the drugs and alcohol, only to develop an addiction to sex work. How would I get out? My friend Kara suggested I check out a massage parlor where the girls screened clients and had tight security. She knew a girl who managed the place and told me I should email her.

At home, I found the paperweight with the picture of my mom inside of it. My mom was about eight years old and wore braids. Her cheeks were lightly freckled and her face held the joy of a just bitten strawberry. Checkered red and white ribbons tied her long braids. She was such a pretty girl.

# 45

"LENNY BRUCE MARRIED A stripper," Adam said as we walked down Hillhurst in Los Angeles in the pouring rain. I'd never dated anyone who wore elbow patches before Adam.

"Lenny Bruce died of an overdose in his hallway," I said.

"That's not the stripper's fault."

I'd met Adam at an AA meeting. He asked if he could interview me about sex work for his podcast. "You're an interesting person," he said. He was an intellectual show-off who tried out his jokes in the meetings whenever he talked. Struggling alcoholics complained about being jobless and suicidal, on the brink of relapsing, while Adam tinkered on his Blackberry.

His gold-flecked green eyes darted around the packed French restaurant. He checked his watch. A frazzled blonde led us to the one available two-top near the window.

Hours earlier, I'd seen my regular client, Blake, who had Parkinson's. I told Adam about him and how he used to be a competitive swimmer but the progression of Parkinson's made him shake and whisper. I told Adam all about my client Dennis who brought me lots of pink, squiggly rubber bands to wrap around his cock. I offered him cock rings, but he liked his grubby rubber bands. During the last ten minutes of our session, Dennis would vibrate if I so much as touched the hairs on his thighs. He'd beg me to stop if my hands touched his legs. I wanted to be completely honest with Adam about what I did with clients, and what I didn't do.

"Do you think you're helping people?" Adam asked.

"I hope so. People are terminally lonely," I said.

His knee jerked and bounced.

I took small bites of warm breadstick dipped in thick, soft butter.

"No show tonight?" I asked.

"I'm as available as you are," he said. He tore a piece of soft bun and dipped it in the butter.

"Most days after about four?"

"My life just got really complicated."

"It's not complicated at all. I'm throwing you the rope of love. All you have to do is grab on," I said. My hand drifted under the table to his thigh. The noise in the room got louder.

"I'm allergic to ropes," he said with his mouth full. The rain fell softly outside. The windows steamed up.

Our steaks arrived. I wanted to tell Adam that
although plenty of men paid me to touch them and go
away, I still wanted intimacy and passion. I wanted to
tell him that sex work was my secret place to be. It was
my *fuck you*. It was my reckless act of despair. It was my, *I
don't need you. Never did*. I could feel wanted and get paid,
yet still walk away unscathed. It helped me pay my bills,
be defiantly self-sustaining, and stay absolutely alone. I
found refuge in clubs where I could hide in the dark,
weigh my options, sit on my hands, and not get high. I
could pull the cash and expose the most hidden parts
of myself without risk. This made me desirable. This
made me powerful. I built a seasoned hustler persona
and body to match. I learned to make easy conversation
about a variety of subjects: football, books, politics, art,
music, and movies. I practiced acting sweet and palatable
even when fear and rage surged through me. I learned
to be strong and unyielding while I spun upside down
and landed in the splits. I exercised the "no" muscle.
*No, I won't meet you later. No, I won't fuck you. No, we're
not dating*. I never, ever dated a client. I wasn't giving
blowjobs, but Adam always asked me anyways.

But the more I told him, the faster he fled. "Your
honesty is suspect," he had said. Adam peeled my skin
back and stripped me in a way the clubs hadn't. I choked
on my vulnerability. I loved him fiercely and courageously
and stupidly. I embarrassed myself. Onstage, he drowned
in his own echoes. He tried out his material on me and
he became the hostile, bitter man his audience expected

him to become while I became a trembling, jealous bully that surprised us both.

"Look," I said. "I want to be considerate of your feelings, but I don't know what they are." I bit into my salty steak. I had always lied about my job, for fear of being left—for fear of compromising. I wanted to be honest. I wanted to be closer to him.

"What?" He motioned to our waitress. Honesty felt like the knife in my hand, cutting through my defenses.

"What are they? Your feelings. What are they?" I squeezed my knife tight. My heart stuck in my throat like a hot stone.

"Can I get some sparkling water please?" he said. The waitress brought Pellegrino and two ice-filled wine glasses.

"You scare me," he said.

"What?" I asked.

The only thing I thought was *fuck*. I watched his rough lips, his chubby hands, his goddamn greedy nipples—the gateway to his hard cock. So many afternoons we spent watching the sun burn after four as the sky turned orange-pink. We fucked. We fucked. We fucked.

The rain stopped.

*Fuck.* I wanted to shield him from the scary bits, from the hideous parts of myself that no one could ever love. But I didn't want to live in my secrets either. I shoved the sweaty money in my pockets. I came and went. I put gas in my car and paid my rent.

"You're going to have to give me some time," he said. I put down my knife and fork, propped my face onto my right palm and stared out the steamy window, beyond naked.

"What is that supposed to mean?" I asked. He gestured to our pretty, thin-boned blonde waitress for the check. I turned red, embarrassed. He checked his phone a few times. He paid, stood, and we left.

As he walked towards his car, I realized there were things I didn't tell him in my quest to be totally honest; like the time he called me from Montreal while I had a client handcuffed to a bed, his ankles tied together with scratchy twine and a dildo in his mouth. I told my client, "I have to get this," and left him tied up to take the call out on the balcony. There was a slight breeze and a full, orange moon, sinking, like a pumpkin just out of reach. His voice made me so happy I could cry. "You sound so far away," I said.

"I'm not that far away." I floated away on his words, breathed in the strong jasmine, and finished my session, feeling something again.

Then, he started calling to disinvite me to his shows. Pulled out of plans last minute. He wouldn't call for days; his texts—when he bothered—looked like Facebook updates for his fans.

I, of all people, should have known that happy endings don't last.

# 46

*I* CLIMB THE FIFTY-FIVE STEPS to the front door of the tantric temple wearing a soft jersey tube dress, leopard-print leggings, and flip-flops. My uniform suggests comfort and allure. It carries the cotton promise of bare shoulders, kundalini poses, and sun-kissed highlights. One shoulder bag is stuffed with freshly folded towels, sheets, pillowcases, and running shoes still moist from the five miles I jogged around the reservoir; the other holds a fifteen-dollar bottle of organic grape seed oil, a package of baby carrots, Trader Joe's spicy hummus, and my computer. I've eaten my egg whites. I smell like vanilla soap and fabric softener.

At step forty, the same number as my age, I pause. I consider tossing the towels in the trashcan below and sprinting away through the alley. I finished grad school, but I've got no book, no teaching job, no agent. I continue up the stairs. My rent isn't going to pay itself.

A civilian might think that the services described on the temple's website—"tantric body work," "sacred temple body work," "body of bliss"—sound like yoga classes, but these are euphemisms for oily massages with happy endings performed by naked chicks wearing feathered earrings.

On the last wooden step, the knot in my neck starts to throb from the climb, and I breathe in heavily. This is the fourth day in a row that I will jerk guys off from 10:00 A.M. till 10:00 P.M. in increments of fifty-minute hours. I drop the bags and fish for my keys to the temple, which is really a modest loft on a residential street in Silver Lake. I look up at the sky. *It's almost over.*

I unlock the front door and step inside. The woman who hired me is standing in the communal kitchen holding a large knife. She cuts a papaya into chunks and crams them into a glass blender with a brown-green paste.

"Good morning," she says. "You have Dragonfly Jay in twenty minutes."

All the clients are assigned nicknames so their real names aren't displayed when we check the temple iPad for our appointments.

"Dragonfly?" I ask, wondering how he earned that name, but the blender whirs and she's already on the phone.

BEFORE THE TEMPLE, IN New Orleans, I was introduced to a woman who gave hand jobs in L.A. She gave me her manager's personal email, and her manager agreed to meet me at a trendily overpriced restaurant on Sunset Boulevard for dinner.

She had short wavy hair and olive-green eyes. Her long legs were muscular, and she wore a strappy leather vest that exposed her boobs. I notice they're organically small, unlike most strippers I've worked with. I asked questions while she sipped Pellegrino out of a wine glass.

"What goes on in sessions?"

She laughed like a giddy bird.

"Every session is different."

I wondered what that meant. I wanted to talk about money.

The temple keeper glanced at the tuna tartare as if she's never skipped a meal or fretted over the cost of dinner. When her salad arrived, she closed her eyes and held her hands in prayer. I watched her, ashamed of my need for cash, because in New Age circles that meant I wasn't abundant. In fact, I was scarcity walking, a pariah, an open mouth needing to be fed.

I snatched up the salty fish and popped it in my mouth. She opened her eyes.

"What exactly do you do in the private rooms?" I asked.

"It's a sensual, sacred bliss massage, ending in a hand release," she said, already bored with the subject.

She had just returned from a yoga retreat in Belize and would much rather giggle about her Belizean boyfriend than talk shop, but all I could think about was making some dough. I needed her to like me. I needed her to trust me enough to grease me up and slip me into the temple so I could stop posting ads on Backpage.com and inviting strangers into my home, where they used my shower and soiled my towels. I needed it so I wouldn't have to hydroplane on bald tires while driving to Camp Pendleton with five bucks in my bank account just to jack off a couple of hostile, drunk Marines on a bed the size of a tampon; so I wouldn't find myself alone when a client pinned me down and shoved his tongue down my throat after I said, "This is going further than I want"; so I wouldn't have to yell in an apartment with claw marks on the walls when I made a client come too fast and he demanded his money back and no one knew where I was. So I wouldn't get arrested again.

At the temple, there were always girls working in other rooms and clients were screened using LinkedIn and Google.

"How much do we pay the house?" I blurted out.

"Eighty dollars for the hour session."

The temple took forty percent of every massage. Clients paid $200 an hour or more, depending on the length and type of massage. This was one swanky jack-off joint.

THE WOMEN I WORK with are dancers, musicians, and transcendental meditators—yoga-sexy former strippers who choose silent retreats over Lady Gaga and Burning Man over camping trips. They tend to reject mascara and bras and don't stay any place for very long. They belly dance, fire breathe, and stilt walk. They talk about chakras and hum. They aren't worried about the LAPD snatching it away because they've never been handcuffed and shoved into the backseat of an unmarked white van in a hotel parking lot after agreeing to give some guy a handjob for $200. They actually believe they're helping men find their higher selves by smearing their balls with coconut oil and making them come.

I quickly learned the temple provides many flavors of handjob. There are handjobs that involve ringing bells, handjobs accompanied by humming, handjobs with guided meditation, and handjobs after deep breathing. Dragonfly Jay has booked a standard "body of bliss" session. For $200, it includes eye gazing, a little light hugging, and...fire breath! Fire breath is a yoga practice in which both hands shoot in the air as if to surrender and breath is held and then spat out in short, violent bursts. It's supposed to activate kundalini energy, which, in New Age yogi terms, is a powerful, dormant, libidinal force located near the tailbone that is supposed to lead to greater orgasms when awakened.

I jerk dudes off in a dark room behind a heavy, gray sliding door. I make a ritual of keeping this room sparkling clean. I sweep dried flowers and balled-up hair from dusty corners and spray the sink with Lysol, pour bleach into the shower until the fumes coat my throat.

I started fetishizing ritual in Catholic school when I would kneel on wooden pews and gaze up at stained glass windows in awe of Jesus' six pack and skinny thighs. I sang songs about blood and lambs while adults in pressed slacks accepted the hot body of Christ.

Here the altar is a shelf adorned with dozens of candles, and instead of Jesus, a statue of the elephant-headed Hindu God Ganesha glares at me from his orange perch. I lift Ganesha and wipe the scarf he sits on with a wet sponge. It leaves a dark smudge.

In the stripper world, I was the queen of Ziploc bags. I'd color-coordinate my clean costumes, then organize them in airtight sets—animal prints in one, pink and white in another, black alone, rhinestone ropes and bracelets separated from fishnet shirts to prevent snags. This compulsion was passed down to me from my mom, who used to organize every single drawer by color and held her chaos together with labels, files, highlighters— the soothing routine of order.

With my client due any minute, there were still candles to place in tiny glass holders and oils to heat in the Crock-Pot. I had to move quickly. I kicked a white tub of antibacterial wipes underneath the massage table so it was hidden from view. I thought about dirty toenails, eczema, sweaty butt cracks, and hairy balls that smell like soggy bread. I looked at my watch and removed my leggings.

MY CLIENT CALLS AS he climbs the stairs to the front door. I turn on the shower and fold the towels into perfect, soft rows, placing them inside a basket. The familiar knot in the left side of my neck aches. On the porch, Dragonfly Jay looks like President Obama: a svelte salt-and-pepper attorney with an elegant, chiseled face and erect posture.

"Hi, I must be Athena," I tease and wrap my arms around him, taking care not to get lipstick on his white shirt. I take his soft hand and lead him into the back room. He removes his polished black shoes outside the door.

"The shower's ready for you," I say.

"I just took a shower, but after those stairs, I could use another," he jokes.

His voice is smooth. When he unbuttons his starchy, long sleeve shirt, my eyes go straight to an extra set of nipples. And while I've seen many men and a lot of nipples, this is the first time I've seen one man with four. I avert my eyes. In this business, it's not a good idea to register shock when a client undresses. I over-smile instead.

I remove my dress and underwear slowly, like in the movies. Dragonfly Jay disappears into the bathroom, emerging a few minutes later. I tell him to lie face down on the massage table.

The more days I devote to the temple, the less time I spend writing and applying to teaching gigs. It's hard to write with a dick in your hand.

I stretch Dragonfly Jay's long, hairless arms between my greasy hands and rub from shoulder to palms. Tranquil drum music fills the room. I slide around the table until I am between his legs. I lie on top of him naked, my belly against his tailbone. My arms are splayed on top of his, as if we are flying. I rub his thighs, calves, feet, and back with gusto. I look at the clock. Twenty-five minutes have passed, so I reach between his legs and touch his balls, lightly—a tease. I slip off the table and whack a golden bell with a wooden stick. It sounds like a soft gong. I massage his head, and my mouth touches his earlobe.

"Ready to turn over?"

"Sure."

"Would you like a pillow?"

"That'd be great."

I drip golden oil onto Dragonfly Jay's thighs like warm maple syrup onto a gingerbread pancake. I stand by his head and reach over his eyes to tweak his accessory nipples. I've read about this birth defect. Usually people get just one extra nipple, but Dragonfly Jay has two. He's special.

"Do you have sensation in these?"

He opens his eyes, two dark pools. "Yes, but not as much." His eyes meet mine. His expression is soft, like the towels folded in the corner.

"You could have a lot of fun with these," I say. "You could pierce them."

I circle the table again and climb on top of it, crouching between his legs, squeezing them.

"I'm not that adventurous," he says.

I wonder if he's married, and if so, does his wife suck his extra nipples? Or does she shy away from them?

Time crawls around my throat. The gray door is locked shut and burgundy curtains shrink the room.

I trickle oil along his cock and press it between my palms, like I'm praying. It jumps. I rub his inner thighs to build up the tension, then stroke slowly. He moans. Curly black hairs fall onto gold sheets and stick to my oily hands. I sigh, knowing I will find them later on the floor and sweep and sponge, but I'll miss a strand or two that will slide into dank corners. When he comes, my legs are under his legs and my boobs are pressed against his thighs. His back is arched, his four nipples hard little cherry pits.

I slither off the table and dunk hot towels into the Crock-Pot of lavender oil. The towels signal it's over. I place them onto his belly, wipe away his come, and then hide the used towels under the table.

"I'll be right back," I say, after placing a pillowcase over his eyes. He will doze while I shower, then it will be his turn to cleanse. Exactly fifty minutes will have passed.

Under the hot water, I scrub the oil from my ribcage with orange, liquid soap and scoot tiny stray hairs into the drain with my toes. I hear soft crying from the next room. I drop to my knees and wash and wash and wash.

# 47

$\mathcal{I}$'M NOT THE TYPE of girl anyone has ever wanted to rescue. Perhaps that's the reason stripper and hooker memoirs disappoint me. They end all neat, tidy, heteronormative, and buttoned up. They end all *Pretty Woman* and diamond-ringed and Pottery Barned, with the damaged girl who finally found Mister Perfect. Mister P fixes her up and buys a house and a puppy and she writes thank you letters on monogrammed stationary.

I don't relate.

I'm not the type of girl who wants to be rescued, but, if I were the brittle girl who longed to land softy in Disney arms, this would be my ending:

You've got soaring self-worth, and you'll never strip again. You'll never even think about it. You've swept the part of you that was for sale under the welcome mat in front of your reformed-whore digs. The transactional psychosexual hard drive of your mind has been erased. You tell yourself this as you cut out your stripper heart. You toss it down the garbage disposal where it howls and you hope Mister P doesn't hear the sound of stripper heart being massacred in your remodeled kitchen.

Down the drain: the night in the San Francisco club where you stripped and fucked a young coke dealer with neck tattoos and a motorcycle helmet for five hundred bucks, just because you felt like it.

Down the drain: The time the man's wife ate your pussy for half an hour while he watched. And you came. Afterwards, you went home to your boyfriend and fucked him.

Down the drain: the hundred lies you told about where you were, what you were doing, who you were with. And those acts that stoked the fire in your pussy that is very hard to put out? Down. The. Drain.

You tell yourself none of it happened. You scratch it away like some other skin. The friends who stood shoulder to shoulder with you in clubs and hotel rooms for years? You erase them.

You walk away with French manicured hands and your husband's American Express card in your purse and forget how your pussy gushed when a wad of sweaty hundreds was shoved into your fist while undulating on a man's boner—while he fantasized about the tip of his cock between your slick lips, probing you like a strobe light, in you, making your spine vibrate.

You deny that you were drunk on their desire for you.

You sprinted out the exit. Left the titty bars in your stripper wake, saved from the big bad sex industry wolf— your self-regard restored. You've found love in the right places. You carry the correct handbag. You are draped in complicated fabrics. You're Snow White now. You're white, you tell yourself. Wiped clean.

And Mom, Mom is proud. We visit, we bake; there is no rush to tell me about the photographs. She calls every other day. "Everything is in bloom! You should see the squash in the boxes. Even my lilies are doing well this year, and the yard is just covered in cherry blossoms and apples. My golden chain is so heavy with blossoms, it looks as if it might just fall over."

THIS IS NOT THAT ending, but here is mine:

The dark bars appear in dreams. I feel them burning holes, trails, sweating through my clothes, forming colonies that climb up my throat and hips, rising heat in my crotch, bursting the threats loose with their pushing. They erected great tents in my blood.

I left the club. It never left me. At the grocery store I see a man's neck and have an impulse to climb up his leg and lick his ear. I watch him open his wallet, and I count the bills out of habit. He looks me in the eye. He looks away, but I keep staring at the cash. Eighty dollars. A hundred. I fight the urge to bend over at the hip and swipe it.

The smell of coconut lotion and bubble gum makes me see red lips, chest, brown nipples, belly jewels; the girl who clenched her asshole onstage to the beat of the music. The one with her locker next to mine whose pupils were big as planets. She made twenty-six hundred dollars one night. *A dancing asshole.* If only I had a dancing asshole. Vanilla, bubble gum, coconut lotion, dance dollars.

The Disney endings are not only written by high-priced gazelles from low places; I've read the same endings in male hustler memoirs. The letdown endings are toweled off and group-therapied. The boys enter fancy rehabs and private schools like a big, fat, outdated, Americana-glazed donut dipped in bullshit-lie.

This is not that. I'm forty years old, still stripping and giving handjobs to pay my rent. I have no clue how to leave this industry and enter the work force. This is the work force. The way out is the way in is the way out.

I thought this would end in the dark, fighting for my life in Los Angeles, three bucks in my pocket, climbing the pole in a seedy bar in Hollywood. Or, I'd get arrested again. I completed the diversion program and graduated grad school and am no closer to a teaching job. This is where I am: I'm still doing this. I will climb out, the window is open a crack, but I don't know when.

HERE IN LOS ANGELES, in the sunlight, my days begin in dirt. I run around a still body of glistening water and swoon at puppies and lazy ducks. It's time to go to work.

I sink into leopard print pillows while the sun stabs golden light on my bare legs. I sit, wait, write, and my phone vibrates. I light up. I whisper to the man on the phone and watch a pot of brown rice simmer. I tell him the address and the door code. After our session, he will be given a password and a nickname and that will be his all-access pass.

Acknowledgments

This book began years ago as shitty, earnest fiction at Antioch's MFA program where my gracious, brilliant mentors pushed me to write nonfiction. I'd like to thank Rob Roberge, an amazing mentor, writer, and friend for his advice and example. I'd like to thank my other mentors at Antioch as well: Dodie Bellamy and Leonard Chang for their feedback and encouragement, and Jim Krusoe at SMCC for demonstrating humility and patience. I want to thank the Citrons for sharing their courage, writing success, and struggles for seven years of lonesome postgrad school Sundays, especially: Xochi-Julisa Bermejo, Jonathan Berzer, Melissa Chadburn, Seth Fischer, Aaron Gansky, Rachel Kann, Trish Paulson, Tisha Reichle, Tina Rubin, Diane Sherlock, and Judy Sunderland. Write On, Citrons!

Thank you to the folks at Rare Bird Lit for giving Spent a birthday and always having my back: Julia Callahan, Angelina Coppola, Tyson Cornell, Alice Marsh-Elmer, and my dreamy editor Seth Fischer.

I'm especially grateful to my wonderful friends who believed in me and this book when I didn't and who offered hope and tenacious encouragement: Greg App: the King of Pleasure, Katya Askar, Shannon Barber, Bella Blue, Laura Bogart, Gayle Brandeis, Hank Cherry, Chiwon Choi, Brittany Davis, Gina Corso, Joe Donnelly, Steve Erickson, Evonne Esparza, Marilyn Friedman and her Writing Pad, Jennifer Grant, Marya Gullo, Silas Howard, Laura Jackson, Linda Jeffers, Bill Jones, Josh Klausner, Heather Luby, Kate Marayama, Anna March, Josh Mohr, Lexie Montgomery, Marty Morgan, Mary Moses, Ruth Nolan, Patrick O'Neil, Lucy O'Reilly, Billy Pitman, David Rocklin, Zoe Ruiz, Jill Soloway, David Spalding (my favorite brain with eyes), Anna Joy Springer, David Henry Sterry, Romy Suskin, Marya Taylor, Michelle Tea, and Lidia Yuknavitch.

Los Angeles offers a tremendously talented writing community to which I am deeply indebted. Although some people may not be named here specifically, many are very much a part of this book. Speaking of my writing community, I'd like to especially thank Steve Almond, Steve Da Jarnatt, and Jerry Stahl for being exemplary writers and great men. I'm also grateful for Dieter Hartmann for his generosity and to Kevin O'Quinn for his initial edits. Thank you Sy Safransky and Luc Saunders at The Sun. It will happen. Wink. Thank you Radar Lab and Squaw Valley Community of Writers for the opportunity to dig in. Big hugs to the Write Girls, especially Brande Jackson and Rachel Kaminer, who taught me to always tell the teenage girls they are amazing because they may have never been told that until now. Tell them.

I am grateful to The Rumpus for their sweet, undying enthusiasm and support, especially Isaac Fitzgerald who has championed my work from the get-go and the amazing Rumpus Women, especially Julie Greicius for holding the rope on the other side of the stream and yelling, "Jump!" I'd like to thank Stephen Elliott and Cheryl Strayed for being brilliant and amazing and kind.

Thank you New Orleans for mothering me when I was broken and for providing the opportunity to work alongside so many complex, bright, beautiful women at Penthouse Club, Ricks Cabaret and Visions.

Thank You, Humboldt County and my family members who still reside there, especially Chuck DeWitt for showing me that we can change the most frightening, awful parts of ourselves and for showing me that change and being that change in the world.

Thank you for loving Mom and showing her mercy, because without mercy, this book would not exist.

Thanks, Mom.